The Peak D
and Tea R

Andrew McCloy

Edited by Ian Johnson

*An independent guide to over 70 cafés
in and around the Peak District*

Johnson Publishing

Published by:
Johnson Publishing
160 Sutton Road, Mansfield
Nottinghamshire NG18 5HH
email: johnson.publishing@virgin.net

First Edition 2003

Text © Andrew McCloy, 2003
Line drawings © Cliff Rowbotham
Photographs © Ian Johnson except for following:
page 24, Masson Mill © Dennis Varty
page 47, shop frontage © Northern Tea Merchants
pages 54 - 56 ©Andrew McCloy

Maps © Ian Johnson

Cover: Cintras Restaurant and Tea Rooms, Hathersage
Back Cover: June Taylor, Three Roofs Café, Castleton

Acknowledgements:
To Cliff Rowbotham for the line drawings.
The numerous café owners for their cooperation and assistance.

ISBN 0-9542574-1-3

Printed by Linney Print Ltd, Mansfield, Nottinghamshire

INTRODUCTION

The novelist Henry James once wrote that there are few hours in life more agreeable than the hour dedicated to the ceremony known as afternoon tea. Whether you've been walking across the Dark Peak moors or cycling the lanes of the limestone dales, pottering about the shops or exploring village churches, there's nothing better than sitting down to a steaming pot of tea and a fresh slice of carrot cake or traditional sponge in a friendly little tea room. Personally, I also enjoy a mid morning visit for the stimulation of fresh coffee; and I've also been known to settle into a corner table with a cheese toastie and a glass of fresh juice over lunch. It's splendidly addictive stuff.

Whether you call them tea rooms or cafés, coffee shops or eateries, the Peak District is blessed with a wide selection of these wonderful places. And perhaps the best thing about them is that they really are so different. In the following pages you will find self-service 'caffs' where tea comes in pint mugs and the all-day breakfast is sufficient to feed a small army. No-one stands on ceremony and no-one leaves hungry. Then at the other end of the spectrum there are the dignified tea rooms, where doilies and bone china and mouth-watering cake stands are the order of the day.

This is a completely independent guide, the establishments listed are the ones we personally have enjoyed and recommend to others. The publisher has not sought, nor received any money from any proprietor. This first-ever Peak District tea room and café guide deliberately sets out to present a wide-ranging and appealing sample of the best establishments the region can offer. We don't limit ourselves to the confines of the Peak National Park (otherwise Ashbourne, Buxton, Matlock and Wirksworth would be left out), but at the same time we have not included every single tea room we have come across. Their inherent variety means that they won't necessarily all have the same appeal to every reader, but half the fun is discovering new places and treating yourself to something different. Who would have thought that some of the best home-baked scones in the Peak District are served in a garden centre coffee shop? Or that quality Fair Trade coffee and original vegan soups are served above a second-hand book shop? Make sure to visit the farm tea room that sells delicious ice cream made from the milk of its own dairy herd; and the Eyam establishment where you can enjoy a slice of Plague Pie and have no detrimental after-effects.

You can find cafés and tea rooms in railway stations (Darley Dale, Hassop and Grindleford), an antique centre (Matlock) and in former mill buildings (Cromford and Cressbrook), as well as a post office (Edensor) and elegant carriage houses (Tissington and Chatsworth). Enjoy a cuppa in an old smithy (Monyash), beside a swimming pool (Hathersage), amid a motorbike showroom (Matlock) and even in the luxurious surroundings of a castle (Willersley at Cromford). For an arty environment go to the Gallery Café in Ashbourne, or if it's books you're after head for Scarthin at Cromford, Scriveners at Buxton, or

Introduction

the Whistlestop Café at Hassop. And if you prefer a more continental café style, perhaps with a touch of the Mediterranean, try the Crown Yard Kitchen at Wirksworth or Treeline at Bakewell.

How to use this guide:

Opening hours are set out as stated by the café owner or manager when we visited, and of course over time this may alter slightly. Most places stay open longer in the summer, and out of season (usually Sept/Oct to Easter) reduce their hours or may even close early if custom is slack. If you want to make sure somewhere is open it's a good idea to call in advance, and if you are bringing a large group then this is especially important.

As regards food, we have tried to give a representative sample from the current menu, including any specials board. Don't necessarily expect it to be available when you visit, although the staples (sandwiches, jacket potatoes, toasties, cakes, etc) are usually a permanent feature of most menus. Some places serve a range of hot, main meals, and whilst this may be available at a few locations all day long, at others it will be limited to set breakfast or lunchtime hours. Also check out the handful of places where the café turns into an evening bistro or restaurant - they are often as good if not better than many pubs for quality of menu and all-round ambience (try the Eyam Tea Rooms, Garden Café at Baslow, Lovers Leap at Stoney Middleton and the Crown Yard Kitchen at Wirksworth).

It goes without saying that tea and coffee is available in all the establishments listed, but check the text carefully if you are after a specialist beverage, since most but by no means all the places serve real coffee and offer a range of unusual teas. For the connoisseur, consider a visit to the likes of Regent House in Matlock, where you can enjoy specialist teas from Kenya, India and China, and rich and aromatic coffee from Central America and the Indian subcontinent. And although it's slightly outside the scope of this particular title, a short drive out of the Peak District along the A619 to Chesterfield reveals the delights of Northern Tea Merchants (see the feature on page 47). For a decent, authentic cup of continental coffee (and not just a lot of frothed milk) visit Cintras at Hathersage or the Crown Yard Kitchen at Wirksworth.

For some entries we state that the cafés or tea rooms have wheelchair access. This is where they have dedicated ramps and adapted toilets, or the facilities are all on ground level and the doorways sufficiently wide. In some instances there are a few steps, and where this is the case it's mentioned.

As far as dogs are concerned, all the establishments listed accept guide dogs inside. A select few welcome other well-behaved dogs, otherwise you will have to leave man's best friend at the door, or sit outside yourself. The same goes for smoking - the majority of places don't allow smoking anywhere inside the premises.

Although cafés and tea rooms don't tend to change hands as often as pubs, the information in this book is obviously subject to change, especially in terms of menus and prices. We cannot be held responsible for any errors or omissions, and if you find any details have changed, or if you have comments or suggestions about places included (or possibly not yet featured), please send them to the address at the front of this book. By the way, if you visit a café as a result of using this guide, please tell the proprietor.

As another of our great novelists, Virginia Woolf, once wrote: one cannot think well, love well, sleep well, if one has not dined well. I hope you enjoy visiting the tea rooms and cafés of the Peak District.

Map showing locations of cafés in this guide

Miles
0 1 2 3 4 5

Place names in black type: Locations of featured cafés

―――――― National Park boundary

―――――― Principal roads

ASHBOURNE - Derbyshire

Ashbourne is a busy market town on the southern edge of the Peak District, and in culinary terms is probably best known for its gingerbread. It is said that the original recipe came from French prisoners of war who were held in Ashbourne during the Napoleonic Wars.

In March the annual Shrovetide 'football match' takes place, causing many shop-keepers to board up their windows. This is a rough and unruly contest between vast scrums of local people in which the aim is to propel a ball towards the opponents' goal - several miles away. There are no defined rules, no pitch of course, and any number of competitors may take part. It's been played every Shrove Tuesday and Ash Wednesday in Ashbourne since the Middle Ages, but no one seems to know why. The Green Man Royal Hotel on St John Street sports one of the last surviving scaffold signs in the country. It spans the width of the main road, and as you might guess from its name was once used as a gibbet. Make sure to visit the attractive market square, where in addition to a decent fish and chip shop you will also find the superb delicatessen, Patrick Brooksbank, which specialises in cheeses, pâtés, puddings and home-made chocolates.

Ashbourne Gingerbread Shop

26 St John Street, Ashbourne.
Tel (01335) 346753
Grid ref: 182467
Open: 8.30-5 Mon-Wed, 8.30-5.30 Thurs-Fri, 8-5 Sat, closed Sun.

Ashbourne Gingerbread Shop

Food: Patisserie choices include cream cakes, puffs, doughnuts and egg custard. Or choose from filled sandwiches and rolls, salads and toasties, through to omelettes, all-day breakfast and Derbyshire oatcakes. See the weekly specials board for other choices, plus children's choices.

Drinks: Filter coffee and cafetières, hot chocolate, and traditional and Earl Grey tea. Cold drinks include milkshakes and Ashbourne mineral water.

General: Housed in a late 15th-century half-timber framed building, there has been a bakery on the premises since 1805, with Birds the Confectioners the latest owners. Ashbourne has long been known for its gingerbread, although unlike the Bakewell Pudding there doesn't seem to be one jealously guarded recipe. The large glass-fronted exterior reveals a take-away bakery counter on one side, and the tea room the other, leading to a lower floor at the back with more seating. The dozen or so tables are all waited upon, and with a low-beamed ceiling it's quite pleasant. Wheelchair access to the front part of the shop, but not to the toilets downstairs. No smoking or dogs inside.

Earth Brand Café, Ashbourne

Earth Brand Café

14 Church Street, Ashbourne.
Tel (01335) 342518
Grid ref: 178466
Open: 10-4 Mon-Fri, 10-5 Sat, 12-4 Sun.

Ashbourne

Food: Toasted bagels and tea cakes, locally-baked cakes, own-brand salad and home-made soups (parsnip and stilton, courgette, broccoli and brie) all prepared fresh in the kitchen. 'On the sunny side up' includes ham and scrambled egg, smoked salmon and scrambled egg, and scrambled egg with feta cheese, while the speciality sandwiches feature Albuquerque Turkey, Neptune's Tuna Feast, and new York Deli Style. The American theme is matched by the generous portions.

Drinks: Coffees include latte, Americano, cappuccino and Espresso con Panna, and can come in cafetières, while speciality teas feature Earl Grey, Ceylon, Pure Darjeeling, Assam and Lapsang souchong. Earth Brand is also licenced to serve beer and wine with meals.

General: Originally an antiques shop, this little gem of a café still has a few odds and ends in the entrance, but go through the inner doors and you will find two small rooms packed with curios including miniature globes, shell pots, toy robots, and American paraphernalia such as baseball gloves and balls, licence plates, etc, that give the place its overall theme. There are only eight tables and it can be a little cramped, but the welcome is warm (table service), and with two fires it's also very cosy in winter. There are also occasional poetry and musical evenings. Children welcome; wheelchair access to front room and newly adapted ground floor toilets; no smoking; dogs at owner's discretion. Named as 'Tea Room/Café of the Year' in the 2002/3 Derbyshire Food and Drink awards.

Gallery Café

Gallery Café

50 St John Street, Ashbourne.
Tel (01335) 347425
www.sjsg.co.uk
Grid ref: 183467
Open: 10-5.30 Tues-Sat, closed Sun.

Food: The menu has a distinctive Mediterranean feel to it - Moroccan chickpea stew, moussaka, home-made hummus, and tapas (in summer) all feature, and it's freshly prepared in the kitchen. "This is not a pasty and chips place," according to the owners. However, there are also open sandwiches, various salads, home-made Spanish omelette, soups, with vegetarian and often vegan options usually available. The cakes are made next door, and you can also choose from the likes of crumpets, muffins, scones and teacakes. Fat-free and sugar-free cakes are also on offer.

Drinks: Coffee comes in a choice of cafetières (Rich Italian, organic, decaffeinated - all from Taylors of Harrogate), plus espresso, latte, cappuccino and Americano. Teas include Earl Grey and fruit choices, plus there's hot chocolate and soft drinks such as freshly-squeezed orange juice and iced tea. The café also has a licence to serve beer and wine.

General: The Gallery Café is located on the first floor of the St John Street Gallery, an elegant, high-ceilinged building that began life as a literary institute, then served as a chapel and later a courthouse. Today it's a smart, contemporary art gallery, featuring a diverse range of canvasses and modern sculpture from local and national artists. The carpeted café is light and spacious, illuminated by huge arched windows with stained glass surrounds, and with trendy modern chairs and tables (with fresh flowers). There are occasional 'jazz suppers', and with table service and a background of gently-piped classical music it's a very civilised and stimulating place in which to relax. No smoking or dogs. Toilets on first floor.

> *"The morning cup of coffee has an exhilaration about it which the cheering influence of the afternoon or evening cup of tea cannot be expected to reproduce"*
> Oliver Wendell Holmes

Spencers the Bakers

Spencers the Bakers

35-39 Market Place, Ashbourne.
Tel (01335) 342284.
Grid ref:179467
Open: 8.30-5 Mon-Sat, 9-5 Sun.

Food: Hot food counter includes roast of the day, fish and chips, all-day breakfast, etc, plus filled sandwiches, salads and ploughman's, jacket potatoes and soups, plus children's choices. Range of cakes and savouries from the bakery counter.

Drink: Cappuccino, Viennese (coffee whipped cream) and espresso in cups, plus cafetières including decaffeinated, Indian Monsoon Malabar AA, and Costa Rica Re Orosi. House tea, Earl Grey and fruit /herbal infusions; and there's also hot chocolate, milk shakes, and a range of other cold drinks.

General: Busy self-service tea room with piped music overlooking the town's old market square. Market days in Ashbourne are Thursday and Saturday, incidentally. Although part of it is a take-away bakery, some of the 16 tables are lined up along the huge, glass-fronted main window, while most are at one end (smoking is allowed in the rear section). There's also a small room upstairs, open at weekends, much more serene with tablecloth covered tables and proper wallpaper. You have to carry your drinks up with you, but the staff will bring hot meals to your table. Toilets on first floor; no dogs. Spencers began selling bread and cakes at their present location in 1908, and now five generations of the family have been baking in Ashbourne. They also have a smaller branch in Wirksworth.

A Potted History of Tea

According to Chinese mythology, the first ever cup of tea was taken by Chinese Emperor Shen Nung, in 2737 BC. Sitting beneath a tree while his servant boiled drinking water, he watched a leaf fall from above and drop into the water. Being an inquisitive sort of fellow, he decided to try the brew. And it just so happened that he was sitting beneath a wild tea tree…

Over the centuries tea became China's national drink, promoted by wandering Buddhists monks. The word 'ch'a' was used to describe tea, while the name itself actually comes from several early Chinese words, such as 'Tchai' and 'Tay', used to describe both the drink and the leaf. In 800 AD Lu Yu wrote the first definitive book on tea, called the 'Ch'a Ching'. It is thought that Arabs may have brought tea to Europe in 850 AD, but it was the Portuguese and Dutch who later brought regular shipments back from the Far East. Sailors and merchants, possibly via the East India Company, introduced tea to Britain, with the first public sales in the 1650s. One of the first to trade tea in Britain was Thomas Garway, who claimed tea was "wholesome, preserving perfect health until extreme old age, good for clearing the sight," plus "it could make the body active and lusty." By the mid 1700s tea had replaced ale and gin as the drink of the masses.

At the 1904 World Trade Fair in St Louis, tea plantation owner Richard Blechynden had planned to give away free samples of hot tea to visitors, but when a heat wave hit no one was interested. In desperation he threw ice into the brewed tea - and it proved such an immediate hit that 'iced tea' entered American culture. Just four years later another important development took place. New York tea merchant Thomas Sullivan began wrapping each sample of tea he delivered to restaurants, and he soon realised that they were brewing the samples in the bags to avoid the mess of tea leaves. Thus the tea bag was born. For more detail see www.teacouncil.co.uk

Bakewell

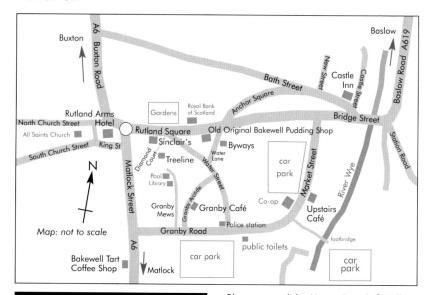

BAKEWELL - Derbyshire

The roadside signs that welcome you to Bakewell proclaim it the capital of the Peak National Park. Perhaps it should also read 'tea room capital', since there are as many as 15 coffee shops and cafés in this small market town - and that's not including the hotels, pubs and wine bars, most of which serve all-day refreshments including teas and coffees. What a choice! You could holiday here for a week and have morning coffee and afternoon tea in a different establishment every day. In between eating and drinking, a wander among the town's shops is also likely to have its diversions. Look out for Charlottes of Bakewell (handmade chocolates) and the Wee Dram (purveyors of fine malt whisky), both on Portland Square.

Bakewell is internationally famous for its pudding - or should that be tart (see main feature)? Whatever it's called, and whichever version you plump for, you'll probably leave Bakewell a few pounds heavier, so walk it off by heading for the beautiful dales and hills of the surrounding countryside.

In addition to the establishments featured below, also look out for the Parakeet Diner (by the town hall, near Rutland Square), the Bakewell Pudding Parlour, Bloomers and the Honey Bun Café (all on Water Street), as well as Gilly's Diner in Hebden Court (off Matlock Street) and the Wye Waters Tea Room near the public library and swimming pool (off Granby Road). Mention must also be made of the tea rooms at Chappell Antiques on King Street and the newly-opened Acorn Café and bistro in King's Court, opposite Chappells. There is also the Farmers Feast Café, situated in the new Agricultural Centre across the River Wye by the main car park. In fact, parking is a problem year-round in Bakewell, and although there are short-stay car parks off Granby Road and by the Co-op stores, your best bet is to follow the signs to the large car park across the River Wye and walk the short distance to the town centre.

Ryan, Bakewell Tart Coffee House

Bakewell Tart Coffee House

Matlock Street, Bakewell. Tel (01629) 814692
Grid ref: 217685
Open: Daily 8-5.30

Food: From breakfast muffins to hot lunches (jacket potatoes and home-made quiches), plus a huge range of savoury and sugary delicacies. Choose between the Traditional Bakewell Slice, Iced Bakewell Slice (soft fondant, and topped by whole almonds), Lemon Bakewell Slice (lemon curd base and fondant) and Moist Bakewell Slice (with coconut). The soups are all made in the kitchen, and accompanied with home-baked rye bread. Also look out for their 'Peak Pasty', a huge pastry concoction of steak, potatoes, swede and carrot with a thick onion gravy.

Drinks: Espresso, latte, cappuccino and mocha coffee, plus cafetières, and hot chocolate with cream and marshallows on top.

General: Situated at the back of the main shop, this is the place for the genuine Bakewell Tart (as opposed to the Bakewell Pudding), which you can either eat in or take away - they come individually or in family and even party size! It's a friendly and popular location throughout the day, and with a limited number of tables you need to get in quick. Guide dogs only; no smoking. Walkers welcome and accessible for wheelchairs, although toilets at rear not adapted.

Byways

Water Lane, Bakewell. Tel (01629) 812807
Grid ref: 217686
Open: 9-4 Mon-Fri, 9.30-4.30 weekends

Food: Choice of sandwiches (standard, special or toasted), jacket potatoes and salads, and 'Byways Speciality Rarebits' - such as Texan (with baked beans), Italian (with spaghetti), Hog (with ham), Woodland (with mushroom) and so on. Apart from the bread everything is made and prepared on the premises, and the ingredients sourced locally, with a particular favourite being Byways own special biscuits - made to a secret recipe, of course!

Drinks: Teas include Earl Grey, Darjeeling, fruit and herb flavours, plus coffee, milkshakes, etc.

General: A first floor location on the corner opposite NatWest bank, the premises was previously a schoolroom and chemists, but for the last 60 years has been a tea room. The four elegant rooms off the main corridor are decorated with paintings and drawings by local artists. One is lit by an open fire in winter (it's very cosy!), and the period fireplaces and variety of old wooden tables and chairs make for an attractive setting. Families and walkers welcome, and toilets available. No smoking and no dogs (except for guide dogs). Inaccessible for wheelchair users.

Granby Café, Bakewell

Granby Café

Granby Arcade, Bakewell.
Grid ref: 217686
Open: 9-5 Mon-Sat, 10.30-4.30 Sun.

Food: Everything is made fresh on the premises - from soups and pasties through to cakes and puddings. There are main meals (hot pots, all day breakfast and stews) through to paninis, toasties, cobs, ploughman's, jacket potatoes, hot and cold sandwiches. Also look out for the daily specials board.

Drinks: Filter coffee and cappuccino / latte /espresso, tea, hot chocolate, Horlicks, etc.

General: A compact, six-table café in the Granby Arcade that links Granby Road with Water Lane in the centre of Bakewell, this bright and welcoming place is popular with locals who enjoy the good food and drink at very reasonable prices. The

Bakewell

new owner has refurbished the premises and rejuvenated the menu, and although the seating is limited it's worth searching out for a decent snack or meal (table service). Wheelchair accessible; no smoking; public toilets nearby; walkers and well-behaved dogs welcome. Parking in nearby pay and display.

Old Original Bakewell Pudding Shop

Old Original Bakewell Pudding Shop

The Square, Bakewell. Tel (01629) 812193
www.bakewellpuddingshop.co.uk
Grid ref: 217686
Open: Daily 9-9 (summer), 9-6 (winter)
Food: Wide-ranging menu features sandwiches and light snacks through to hot meals such as roast of the day, steak and stout pie, filled Yorkshire puddings, lamb and apricot cobbler, and Blacksmith's Skillet (black pudding, bacon, mushroom and onion). Pies, bread, scones and puddings all made on the premises, and own range of pickles and chutneys also very popular. Take-away counter downstairs in shop (filled rolls, fresh bread, Bakewell Puddings, etc).
Drinks: Speciality teas and coffees, including cappuccino, and a variety of cold drinks. The premises are fully licenced.
General: This busy and popular establishment lays claim to the original Bakewell Pudding recipe (see separate feature), and puddings are certainly the star attraction. They're made on the premises and sold in the well-stocked shop downstairs (where the staff wear period costumes), or you can even 'post a pudding' if you feel the urge. Occasional tours

of the bakehouse also take place, and look out for the collection of odd and eccentric teapots in the downstairs back room. Here you will also find the shop's own range of pickles, jams, chutneys and mustards. The spacious first floor restaurant (with seating for up to 90) was sympathetically refurbished in early 2003, with original beams uncovered and the original feel of the old building restored. But don't overlook the specially made carpet, incorporating a pudding design! High chairs and baby-changing facilities available, plus sumptuous toilets. No dogs except guide dogs; no smoking.

Lucy, at the Old Original Bakewell Pudding Shop

> "The British have an umbilical cord which has never been cut and through which tea flows constantly. It is curious to watch them in times of sudden horror, tragedy or disaster. The pulse stops apparently, and nothing can be done, and no move made, until 'a nice cup of tea' is quickly made. There is no question that it brings solace and does steady the mind. What a pity all countries are not so tea-conscious. World peace conferences would run more smoothly if 'a nice cup of tea', or indeed, a samovar were available at the proper time"   Marlene Dietrich

Bakewell Pudding or Bakewell Tart?

There is much confusion, conjecture and downright snobbery when it comes to Bakewell's famous gastronomic creation. Most locals will tell you that it's properly a pudding, and not a tart, and several establishments lay claim to the original recipe. It's even claimed to be locked away in someone's safe!

Legend has it that the so-called Bakewell Pudding originated in the Rutland Arms, Bakewell's handsome Georgian hotel that overlooks the main square and which was previously called the White Horse Inn. Its recipe is attributed to a Mrs Greaves, probably the wife of the first proprietor, who in the mid 1800s came up with a mixture of egg yolks, clarified butter and fine sugar "...poured upon the preserve in a puff paste". Later almonds or almond flavouring was added. But there is another version to the story, which has one of her hapless cooks pouring the egg mixture not into the pastry as she should have done but over the strawberry jam instead. The tart inadvertently became a pudding, but it proved so popular that they decided to make it again. Inevitably the recipe's fame spread locally, and one story goes on to relate how Mrs Wilson, a local candlemaker's wife, soon began a successful baking business centred on the pudding from her cottage by the Square (now home to the 'Old Original Bakewell Pudding Shop').

Whatever the origin, you will find home-made Bakewell Puddings - and Bakewell Tarts - in most of the tea rooms throughout Bakewell, and depending on the sweetness of your tooth you will probably not be disappointed whatever version you try.

For a fuller account of the great Bakewell Pudding saga see 'Mrs Ann Greaves & the Bakewell Pudding' by Trevor Brighton (Bakewell & District Historical Society, 2000), available in the local tourist information centre and Bakewell Bookshop.

Sinclairs Coffee Shop

The Square, Bakewell. Tel (01629) 814164
Grid ref: 217685
Open: 9-4.30 Mon-Sat (summer), 9-4 (winter), closed Sun.

Food: Range of hot and cold snacks and meals, including toasted sandwiches, jacket potatoes, soup and hot paninis (including grilled Mediterranean vegetables, ham and brie with tomato). The home made quiches, sausage meat lattice pie and Welsh rarebit are all popular, and puddings and cakes include Victoria Sandwich Cake. Lunches served from 11.30-3.30, followed by afternoon teas and cream teas.

Drinks: Usual range of teas and coffees (filter coffee top-ups half price) and licenced for wine.

General: An elegant, first floor establishment above Sinclairs modern and classic china sales (you have to go through the shop to reach the stairs), which includes a Royal Crown Derby gallery in the basement. Small but comfortable, with customer toilets. No smoking, and no dogs. At the top of the stairway you are faced with a striking Elizabethan 'overdoor' made for a porch by an unknown Dutch sculptor, almost certainly working for the Duke of Rutland's Haddon Estate at the time - notice the carved Jacobean dress and arms of England and France.

Overdoor - Sinclair's Coffee Shop

"You can tell when you've passed into Germany because of the badness of the coffee." King Edward VII

Bakewell – Bamford

Treeline

Diamond Court, Water Street, Bakewell.
Tel (01629) 813749
Grid ref: 217685
Open: Daily 10-5 (summer), 10-4, 10-5 week ends (winter), closed Thurs from Jan-March.

Food: From sandwiches and salads, croissants and pastries, through to soups and hot specials, all prepared on the premises. There are vegetarian options, such as spinach and ricotta cheese pancakes and spinach and hazelnut lasagne, while hot panini fillings include turkey, cranberry sauce and brie, and tandoori chicken, mint yoghurt and cucumber.

Drinks: Filter coffee, espresso, cappuccino, and so on, plus speciality teas, and wine.

General: This attractive, modern-looking 'eatery' (as they describe it) is tucked away by a quiet, vine-covered courtyard between Rutland Square and the swimming pool/library. The outside seats are popular in summer, and inside the light wood floor and trendy stools and tables give it an urban and even slightly continental feel. A touch of the Mediterranean in Derbyshire, perhaps? The adjacent craft shop and gallery includes furniture, carvings, jewellery, ceramics, paintings and textiles from artists and craftsmen and women from the Peak District and beyond. The eatery is accessible to wheelchairs, but the toilets are upstairs. No smoking or dogs inside.

Upstairs Café

Market Street, Bakewell. Tel (01629) 815567
Grid ref: 219685
Open: 9.30-4.30 Mon-Sat, 10.30-4.30 Sun

Food: Varied and mouthwatering menu, featuring toasties, salad platters, sandwiches, soup, jacket potatoes, Provençette (hot toasted baguettes) and 'house favourites' such as brie, bacon and cranberry melt, spicy meatballs, and homity pie. There are numerous cakes and pastries, and puddings like orange and rhubarb crumble, and blueberry crumble. Look out for the changing specials board, which can include the likes of Thai chicken, tortilla wrap, quiche and cannelloni.

Drinks: Coffees include double espresso Macchiato (with foamed milk) and Con Panna (with whipped cream), plus hot chocolate, milkshakes, smoothies, flavoured cappuccinos and latte, and organic teas. Reduced price for filter coffee refill.

General: Stylish, spacious and decidedly upmarket, this clean and comfortable café which opened in 2000 shares its first floor premises with a gift store, and is situated above the Original Farmers Market Shop on the corner of Market Street and Granby Road, opposite the Co-op supermarket. Wicker chairs and tasteful lighting give the place a relaxed feel, and everyone from families to walkers are welcome. Toilets to the rear; high chair available. No smoking and no dogs (except guide dogs).

Upstairs Café, Bakewell

BAMFORD - Derbyshire

The Bay Tree Coffee Shop is part of the High Peak Garden Centre, which is located not strictly speaking in the village of Bamford, but off the A6187 Castleton Road in the Hope Valley.

Bay Tree Coffee Shop

High Peak Garden Centre, Bamford.
Tel (01433) 651250
Grid ref: 204827
Open: Daily 10-5, (not open when garden centre closed)

Food: The menu includes the usual soup and sandwiches, plus bacon butties and BLTs, but here look out for the range of

delicious scones, sponge cakes and short-bread, all of which are made fresh on the premises to a very high quality. Scones come in various flavours (apple, sultana, date and apple, cheese and banana) while the shortbread may include plain, cherry and choc chip. Also on the list: millionaire slice, fudge flapjack, domino, coffee and walnut flapjack, and so on.
Drinks: Twinings Select and Specialist teas, including herbal and fruit infusions, milk shakes, milk and honey, hot chocolate. The Bay Tree blends its own coffee (a Blue Mountain blend), which is also on sale in packets. For diners it comes in cups (with free refills) and cafetières, plus Viennese, cappuccino, Americano, mocha, espresso and latte are all available.
General: The open plan, single roomed building is pleasant if not especially remarkable, although the large windows make it light and airy, and look out over the array of trellises, bird baths, tubs and pots of the garden centre. However, the walls surrounding the ten tables act as a gallery for local artists - all the prints, photographs and paintings are for sale. Walkers are welcome (there's an outdoor gear shop next door); and the coffee room and its toilets are accessible for wheelchairs. No smoking or dogs inside, and no outside seating. Large free car park.

Garden Café, Baslow

Garden Café

Church Street, Baslow. Tel (01246) 582619
Grid ref: 253724
Open: Daily 9-5.30 (evening restaurant Fri and Sat evenings)
Food: From breakfast and brunch (scrambled egg with smoked salmon, cinnamon toast, etc) through to day-time meal and light snacks, breads and pastries, soup and jacket potatoes, and the likes of toasted goats cheese on ciabatta. Most of the food is made on the premises, such as soups (broccoli and stilton, celery, carrot and coriander) and main meals like liver and onions and fresh fish and chips. For afternoons there's a selection of cream teas and cakes.
Drinks: Full range of specialist teas and coffees, as well as cold drinks.
General: Awarded 'Best Tea/Coffee House of the Year' in the Derbyshire Quality in Food and Drinks Award 2001/2, and a finalist in the 'Heart of England Food and Drink Excellence Awards 2002', this stylish café at the end of a short parade of shops opposite the church is a comfortable and welcoming place. Attractively furnished (look out for the stylish lamps and mirrors), it has a parquet floor and interesting prints, an open fire in winter, and there's outside seating front and back. All on ground level, including the toilets out the back, so it's accessible for wheelchairs. No smoking or dogs inside. Walkers welcome. The café is next door to (and part of) Avant Garde, which specialises in design led accessories for the home and garden; and on Friday and Saturday evenings the café turns into a popular restaurant for á la carte dining. Limited parking in lay-by opposite.

BASLOW - Derbyshire

This is a rather strung-out village, straddling the A619/A623 junction north of Chatsworth. Around the triangular green at what is known as Nether End (off the Chesterfield to Sheffield road) you'll find the Café on the Green, plus you can get daytime refreshments in the elegant surroundings of the Garden Room at the nearby Cavendish Hotel. The other main centre is clustered about the parish church of St Anne, with its unusual clock face, near the delicate medieval bridge across the River Derwent (look out for the tiny toll booth by its side). Opposite this is the Garden Café, while across the bridge the riverside lane through Bubnell provides a much quieter stroll to walk off those chocolate cake calories.

Baslow – Buxton

Café on the Green

Nether End, Baslow. Tel (01246) 583000
Grid ref: 258723
Open: 9.30-5 Mon-Sat (summer), 9.30-4.30 (winter), 9-5.30 weekends all year round.

Food: Full range of meals and snacks, from bacon and stilton melts and sausage cobs through to popular main meals such as roast of the day, lamb pies, stew in Yorkshire puddings, etc. Choice of sandwiches and hot paninis, all prepared in the kitchen, as well as jacket potatoes, salads and soups. Breakfast board 'till late morning/midday, plus a range of cakes and desserts.

Drinks: Filter and other coffees, plus fruit teas, Early Grey, Darjeeling, etc.

General: Refurbished in 2003, this self-service tea room off the green at Nether End used to be called the Goose Green Tea Rooms, and is popular with visitors who enjoy the easy riverside path through to Chatsworth. Because of the large shop-front windows it's quite bright, with a fully tiled floor, 12 tables (inside only) and upstairs toilets. (There are public toilets with disabled access across the green.) No smoking and no dogs. Hosts occasional art exhibitions. Large pay and display car park across the green.

BUXTON- Derbyshire

Famous for its thermal springs, the Romans called Buxton 'Aqvae Arnemetiae' (the Spa of the Goddess of the Grove), and ever since then people have come to this high Derbyshire town to take the waters. The springs are believed to be anything up to 5,000ft underground, and they remain at a constant 28°C (82°F). You can taste the pure, if tepid water, as it streams unceasingly from St Anne's Well on the Crescent. It's perfectly safe to drink, and indeed many local people, including the author, regularly fill up plastic bottles full of the life enhancing Adam's Ale completely free of charge. Alternatively, you can go into the supermarket and pay a lot of money for the same.

Opposite the well is the handsome Crescent, designed by John Carr of York, and other must sees in Buxton include the Edwardian Opera House, home to the annual International Gilbert & Sullivan Festival, and the recently renovated Pavilion Gardens. Up on the hill is the former Royal Devonshire Hospital, whose grand, unsupported dome is 118 feet high and 154 feet across and was the widest in Europe, when it was built in the 1850s. The building is set to be part of the University of Derby's new Buxton campus. The influx of students should give a boost to the town's cafés and pubs.

Hargreaves Coffee Shop

16-18 Spring Gardens, Buxton.
Tel (01298) 23083
Grid ref: 059736
Open: 9.30-4.30 Mon-Sat, closed Sun.

Food: Breakfast served 'till 11.30, with full English including black pudding and oatcake. Light snacks feature toasties and cheese/eggs/beans on toast, plus there's open sandwiches (try the cottage cheese, apple and sultana) and jacket potatoes. Apart from the daily specials board main selections include lasagne, pasta bake, gammon, Cumberland sausage. Meanwhile, the 'Kids Menu' skips the burgers and in a welcome change offers instead half jacket potatoes (with optional filling) and one slice of toast with cheese or beans or scrambled egg, plus there's a 'Kids Lunch Box' available too. Among the cakes and desserts are apple pie, carrot cake, cappuccino cake and chocolate fudge cake.

Drinks: Choice of English breakfast or speciality tea, including lemon tea; while there's cups, pots or mugs of filter coffee, plus cappuccino, espresso, double espresso, and latte. Also hot chocolate with cream, fresh milkshakes and Buxton mineral water.

General: This first floor coffee shop is above Hargreaves & Sons, which since 1906 has been run by four generations of the same family (it sells souvenir plates, crockery and gifts), and maintains the style of the two-room Edwardian showroom in which it is housed. The richly patterned, period wallpaper complements the huge mirrors, high ceilings and lace covered tables. There are two huge glass show cases, rescued from a Manchester store in 1913 and now displaying ceramics and memorabilia. Look for the old prints on the walls, including black and white portraits of the former family members who have run the business. Partly self-service, there is seating for around 50, with toilets at the rear. No smoking and no dogs. Limited parking in streets behind.

Hydro Café Tea Rooms

75 Spring Gardens, Buxton. Tel (01298) 72193
Grid ref: 062736
Open: 9.30-5 Mon-Sat, 10.30-4.30 Sun.
Food: Breakfast menu includes scrambled egg, bacon and tomatoes on a Derbyshire oatcake, and hot bacon muffin, while light meals feature soup, Welsh Rarebit, hot toasted sandwiches, jacket potatoes and salads. Hot main meals range from chilli and fish to pasta bake, with a daily special and vegetarian option always available. From the 'traybakes and desserts' list there's scones, crumpets, shortbread, carrot and walnut cake, and traditional favourites such as treacle sponge and custard. Also serves authentic Bakewell Puddings. Decent sized portions.
Drinks: Yorkshire Tea, plus Earl Grey, Darjeeling, camomile and peppermint. Filter coffee by cup (free top-ups) or cafetiere, including decaffeinated, cappuccino and espresso as well.
General: Large, light and open plan tea room towards the bottom of Buxton's pedestrianised Spring Gardens. Seating for 60 inside, and 20 outside in the summer. Fully carpeted and with prints of old Buxton around the walls, it has a traditional and homely feel and is evidently popular with local shoppers. Table service, and foot tapping jazz and Big Band piped music at just the right volume. Smoking permitted at rear; no dogs, except guide dogs. Prams and wheelchairs welcome, despite slight front step, but toilet door too narrow for wheelchairs. Pay and display car park to rear.

No 6 The Square, Buxton

No 6 The Square

6 The Square, Buxton. Tel (01298) 213541
Grid ref: 057735
Open: 10-6 Mon-Sat (summer), closed Sun, 10-4/5 Tues-Sat (winter)
Food: Morning menu 'till noon includes muffins, cinnamon toast, crumpets, and oatcake wraps with crispy bacon. At midday the main meals include home made soup, quiche, open and closed sandwiches (such as crispy bacon, mushroom and red onion, Dove Dale Blue cheese and apple), as well as choices from a daily specials board. Much of the produce comes from Chatsworth Farm Shop. 'Afternoon Tea' comprises smoked salmon, cucumber and cream cheese, fruit scones with jam and clotted cream, No 6 cakes, and a pot of speciality tea.
Drinks: Choose from filter coffee, cappuccino, espresso, latte and mocha, and hot chocolate with fresh whipped cream. Then there's Yorkshire Tea, and various varieties from Taylors of Harrogate: Assam, Darjeeling, peppermint, Earl Grey, camomile or peach.
General: A refined and tasteful tea room almost opposite the Opera House and Pavilion Gardens, No 6 is fronted by elegant arches. Inside are two high-ceilinged rooms with wicker chairs and high class paintings and prints, a real open fire and shiny pine floor. Newspapers are available for browsing. Bonsai trees and palms

Buxton

complement the real flowers that adorn each table, and look out for the teapot collection around the picture rail. Table service throughout, including tables placed outside in summer. Despite the front step the tea rooms and the ground floor toilets are wheelchair accessible. No smoking, no dogs inside. Walkers welcome.

Mary's Wine Bar, The Old Hall Hotel, Buxton

The Old Hall Hotel

The Old Hall Hotel, near the Opera House and Pavilion Gardens, is another popular venue for morning coffee and afternoon tea - despite owning and running the nearby tea rooms known as No 6 The Square. The original Old Hall was built by the Earl of Shrewsbury in 1550, and received many famous guests. Mary, Queen of Scots, stayed several times and in 1584 she was there for the last time, and as a captive. It is reputed that she scratched a message on a window; "Buxton, whose warm waters have made thy name famous, perchance, I shall visit thee no more, farewell!" The present hotel dates from 1670. Today food and drink is served in Mary's Wine Bar between 9am-11pm, but it can also be taken into the two front lounges (one smoking and one non-smoking). As well as main meals there's an afternoon tea menu featuring sandwiches, scones, tea-cakes and sweets, with various organic teas and speciality coffee from Matthew Algie (including 'Ristretto', a double espresso at half the size). Wheelchair accessible. Popular with walkers. The Old Hall Hotel is located on The Square, Buxton, tel (01298) 22841.

Web site; www.oldhallhotelbuxton.co.uk

Pavilion Gardens

The 23 acre Pavilion Gardens were established in 1871, and thanks to a recent £3.3m Lottery grant the grounds have been restored to their former glory with a boating lake, ornamental flower beds and miniature train. Between April and September bands perform every Sunday at the bandstand on the promenade, and inside the Gardens complex there are shows and meetings all through the year - including W.I. and Farmers Markets, Country and Western evenings, antique and record fairs, plus an annual brass band festival. Also make sure to visit the splendid conservatory adjoining the restaurant, fully temperature controlled to support a range of flowers and plants (and a pond of Koi carp) that would otherwise be absent in England's highest market town – the little matter of 1,100ft above sea level.

Pavilion Gardens Coffee Shop

St John's Road, Buxton. Tel (01298) 23114
Grid ref: 056736

Open: Daily 10-5 (summer), 10-3 (winter, weekends only).

Food: The Coffee Shop serves sandwiches and rolls made on the premises, freshly prepared soup, plus sausage rolls and pastries and a selection of locally-made cakes and biscuits. The Promenade Restaurant downstairs has a good choice of hot meals (including fish and vegetarian options) every lunchtime throughout the week, while the adjoining self service cafeteria has ice creams, drinks and light snacks to eat in or take away.

Drinks: Speciality coffee includes Americano, latte, espresso, café crème and cappuccino, and teas include Earl Grey, Darjeeling, peppermint and various fruit infusions. Cold drinks include Buxton mineral water (of course!).

General: This long, rambling, Victorian complex above the park and gardens, with its high glass windows and roofs, features an all-day cafeteria and lunchtime only restaurant (both open year round), plus a coffee shop open daily in the summer but weekends only in winter. All three venues are no-smoking and have a large number of tables, which is just as well since it can get very busy in the summer. The self service Coffee Shop is arranged around a wide, square balcony on the first floor (no disabled access, but toilets on ground floor), with views down to the restaurant below as well as out over the leafy park. It's spacious and comfortable, and with the huge glass windows, wide staircases and bench lined promenade outside, it almost has a seaside feel to it (an unusual sensation in landlocked Derbyshire). No dogs inside the Pavilion, but take-away food, drinks and ice creams are available from the cafeteria.

Scriveners Bookshop, Buxton

Scriveners Bookshop

Located on the High Street in what's known as Higher Buxton, Scriveners is a bookworm's paradise! Also specialising in bookbinding and restoration, it has around 30,000 second-hand books spread over five floors (including the basement), ranging from pulp to antiquarian, childrens to collectables. There's a 'Saturday Café' on the second floor, with table served tea, filter coffee and cakes, but at other times it is free self-service of tea and instant coffee. Although the 'café' only has three tables and a settee, there are others chairs dotted around most rooms, and it goes without saying that browsers are welcome. The shop is open 9-5 Mon-Sat, 1-4.30 Sun, all year round, tel (01298) 73100.

CALVER- Derbyshire

Pronounce it 'carver' and you'll be one step ahead of the rest. Either way, work up an appetite with a walk alongside the River Derwent between Calver and Froggatt, or better still stride out along Curbar Edge, an eye catching gritstone outcrop that runs along the high eastern edge of the valley (there's a car park at the top of the lane at Curbar Gap if you don't fancy the walk up). Near the craft centre at Calver Bridge is Calver Mill, a large and rather severe looking former cotton mill. It has recently been converted into private apartments, and has previously been used as a set for the 1970s TV series 'Colditz'.

> *"Never trust a man who, when left alone in a room with a tea cosy, doesn't try it on."*
> Billy Connolly

Eating House

Calver Bridge, Calver. Tel (01433) 631583
Grid ref: 247746
Open: Daily 9-5.30.
Food: Breakfast served 9-11.30, including scrambled egg and salmon, bagels, etc. Changing blackboard menu includes hot meals like roast beef, Tuscan vegetable casserole, curry, sausage and mash, etc, and lighter snacks such as baguettes, sandwiches and jackets potatoes. Pies (leek and potato, homity pie) and salads (warm Greek, prawn, Caesar) are particularly popular. Plenty of mouth-watering cakes and tea-time choices: scones, tea bread, Eccles cakes, lemon meringue pie, shortbread. Main meals and most of snacks made on premises.
Drinks: Filter coffee (free top-ups), cappuccino, latte, mocha, plus specialist teas and herbal/fruit infusions. Also, fruit juices, pressé, and other cold drinks.
General: The tea room is accessed via the Derbyshire Craft Centre at Calver Bridge (off the A623 Baslow Road), an extended craft shop selling pottery, local crafts, toys, books, etc, and including a children's playroom. An L-shape arrangement at the end of the building, the self-service Eating House is smallish but not cramped, a clean and comfortable place with exposed stonework and a tiled floor (so walkers

have no need to remove boots). There are handsome wooden bench seats, newspapers for browsing, and an outside seating area provides for dogs and smokers. A ramp provides wheelchair access to the car park, but not to the indoor toilets which involve several steps. Car park for Craft Centre and café customers.

Outside Café

Baslow Road, Calver Sough. Tel (01433) 639571
Grid ref: 239748

Open: 9.30-4.30 Mon-Fri, 9-5 weekends for last hot food orders, but drinks and cakes usually served for extra half hour every day.

Food: Wide ranging blackboard menu, including paninis, sandwiches (cold and toasted) and jackets spuds, home-made soup and salads. There are hot meals such as fish, gammon, pies, toad in the hole, and light snacks on toast, all in decent sized portions. If you're after a hearty meal to start the day try the full or vegetarian breakfast, hot breakfast sandwiches, or the scrumptious Kinderstack - sausage, bacon, mushrooms, beans and egg stacked on four slices of toast or three rosti. All the meals are cooked to order and the food is sourced locally wherever possible.

Drinks: Filter coffee, hot chocolate, milk shakes and smoothies, plus tea (in pots or mugs - including pint mugs), with herbal and fruit infusions.

General: This light, airy café on the crossroads at Calver Sough is part of (and run by) the Outside store, a popular walking and climbing shop. It's clean, bright and modern, and although it's especially popular with outdoor types ("muddy boots definitely welcome!") there is plenty of local and passing trade that drops by. Newspapers to browse; high chair available - and all meals are available half-size, half-price for children. The shop and café are both wheelchair accessible (including toilets). Dogs welcome by picnic bench seating outside; no smoking inside. Car park for shop and café customers.

> *"Coffee in England is just toasted milk."*
> Anon

Castleton and the Hope valley are popular destinations for visitors to the Peak National Park, not least for the variety and sheer beauty of the landscape. It's where the pearly white limestone dales of the White Peak give way to the high and harsher Dark Peak, characterised by the boggy upland moors of Kinder Scout and Bleaklow.

Across the valley from Castleton is the unmistakable bulk of Mam Tor (1,695 ft), and from here a stunning (and comparatively easy) ridge walk heads east to Lose Hill, with impressive views across Edale towards Kinder Scout. Immediately above the village stands the Norman ruins of Peveril Castle, from where Castleton's medieval gridiron street layout becomes apparent. It's a steep pull up to the top, so don't try and race anyone half your age.

If all this talk of heights is making you giddy why not explore underground instead? Castleton's famous showcaves and caverns include Speedwell Cavern, dug by miners over 200 years ago and now explored by means of a subterranean canal boat, and Blue John Cavern, named after the semi-precious variety of fluorspar found there. Peak Cavern has one of the largest cave entrances of any in the country, and its height and damp atmosphere were once exploited by rope-makers who established cottages and even an ale house at its entrance.

Old Nags Head

Cross Street, Castleton. Tel (01433) 620248
Grid ref: 152829
Open: Daily 9-9.

Food: The all-day menu features sandwiches, jacket potatoes, salads and omelettes, as well as a standard range of hot main meals such as steak and ale pie, giant filled Yorkshire puddings. The Sunday carvery is also very popular. From 6-9 the evening menu is also served, featuring more select main dishes. Also look out for the blackboard choices of cakes and puddings, including strawberry jam pudding, lemon sponge with lemon sauce, treacle pudding and fruit crumble. Most of these are made locally or in their own kitchen.

Drinks: The specialist 'bean to cup' coffee machine provides freshly ground coffee to order, either for proper glass cups of espresso, mocha, cappuccino, latte, etc, or cafetières. Speciality teas include varieties from Twinings, decaffeinated and Tetley's Earl Grey. The premises are also fully licenced.

General: Built in the 18th century, and a former coaching inn, the hotel has two large and quite elegant open rooms that overlook the main street. Both are comfortable and carpeted with high ceilings, vast windows, and can seat as many as 60 people in total. Table service; piped music. Smoking and dogs allowed in the bar area only. Limited parking in road at side, or pay and display car park nearby.

Rose Cottage Café

Cross Street, Castleton. Tel (01433) 620472
Grid ref: 150829
Open: Daily 10-5, closed Fri. Also closed in Jan and Feb.

Food: Fresh and toasted sandwiches, freshly made soup and rolls; children's meals; plus home-made pies, scones and desserts. Hot meals include gammon, pies, chilli, fish, egg and chips, etc, and breakfast served until 11.30. There are also set cream teas, and the wide choice of cakes includes lemon and sultana, carrot, mandarin and almond, coffee, lemon curd, and date and walnut. They are all home-made in the café, with the exception of the chocolate fudge ("we are still trying to perfect that one!"). Locally produced Bradwells ice cream is also served.

Drinks: Apart from the regular filter coffee, speciality coffee includes cappuccino and cappuccino grande ("more steamed milk for a milder flavour"), espresso, latte, Americano, and macchiato - "small, strong coffee with a delicate first impression created by placing a small amount of foamed milk on top of the cream".

General: Popular self-service café run by the same family for 36 years, situated in extended, open plan cottage on the main street. Tastefully lit and fully carpeted, the

cosy interior can seat up to 60, with the lure of the cake stands at the main counter the natural focus. Meanwhile, the quiet and sheltered patio at the rear holds a further six tables in summer. Reasonably wheelchair accessible, the toilets are at the far side of the patio. Smoking and dogs permitted inside.

June Taylor of Three Roofs Café, Castleton

Three Roofs Café

The Island, Castleton. Tel (01433) 620533
Grid ref: 148829
Open: 10-5 Mon-Fri, 9.30-5.30 weekends.

Food: Comprehensive menu that includes main meals (all-day breakfast, fish and chips, gammon, giant Yorkshire puddings), jacket potatoes, hot and cold baguettes, and blackboard specials such as stews, home-made pies and pancakes. Long list of home made cakes and desserts include the likes of cherry and almond flapjack, farmhouse tea bread, apple pie, hot Belgian waffle, lemon drizzle cake and brownies. All the main meals are prepared fresh in the kitchen, and the owner is planning to introduce some traditional Derbyshire fare to the menu, based on traditional recipes.

Drinks: Pots of tea include Yorkshire, Earl Grey, Ceylon, Darjeeling, Assam and Camomile, plus fruit and herbal infusions, while filter coffee comes in cups (50p refill) or cafetières, and also features chocolate latte (hot whipped milky chocolate).

General: Long, narrow building, opposite

Castleton – Chatsworth

entrance to Castleton's main car park, which was originally a farm but has been a café for the last 30 years. Table service throughout; the 15 or so glass topped tables are surrounded by prints and picture rail displays of decorative plates and teapots. No dogs or smoking inside, but a few tables outside, and in the summer a regular stream of ice creams is dispensed via the window hatch. Walkers are certainly welcome, despite the carpet. High chairs are available. The café is accessible for wheelchairs, but the door to the inside toilets is narrow (public toilets with disabled access, in car park opposite).

> *"If this is coffee, please bring me some tea; but if this is tea, please bring me some coffee."* Abraham Lincoln

CHATSWORTH - Derbyshire

A mecca for visitors to the Peak District, Chatsworth is one of the finest stately houses in the country, beautifully sited above the River Derwent amid 1,000 acres of rolling deer park and steep, wooded hillsides. The house has been much altered since its Elizabethan beginnings, and it now contains an array of impressive gardens that include amongst other things a cascading waterfall, various fountains and a traditional maze. The Carriage House Restaurant sounds grand, indeed looks grand, but is in fact simply a posh self-service cafeteria. It's located just up from the main house, off the beautiful and spacious courtyard, on the opposite side of which is the elegant Jean-Pierre's Bar, a licensed café bar with table service. In addition to this, there's a café at the nearby children's farm and adventure playground, and at the garden centre (see below); plus the Stud Pantry at Chatsworth Farm Shop a mile to the north of the house (see under Pilsley). For full details of activities and visitor services at Chatsworth call 01246 565300 or visit the web site at www.chatsworth.org

The Courtyard, Chatsworth

Carriage House Restaurant

Chatsworth. Tel (01246) 565300
Gird ref: 263703
Open: Daily 10.15-5.30 (Apr-Dec), and when House is open.

Food: Cold snacks such as sandwiches, quiche and salad (including pork pie, salmon, vegetarian and trout) through to hot meals (pasties, pasta, sausages), soup, jacket potatoes, etc. Always a couple of daily hot specials. Cakes and desserts may include trifle, gateau, scones, chocolate torte, melon, and cream caramel.

Drinks: Cups and pots of filter coffee, including decaffeinated, and speciality Twinings tea. Cold drinks feature iced tea and speciality apple and pear juice; and because the restaurant is licenced a range of wines and beers.

General: Seating up to 250, the tastefully converted Carriage House was built in the 1840s by the 6th Duke, and on a low balcony towards the rear contains a handsome stagecoach that was brought to Chatsworth in the 1890s and was used by the present Duke and Duchess and their son at the coronation of the Queen in 1953. Despite its grandeur and size, the place is often packed with visitors, and queues can form at particularly busy periods. The toilets have been adapted for wheelchairs and have baby changing facilities. No dogs or smoking inside the self-serving restaurant. There is a modest car parking charge for visitors to Chatsworth, but since the lovely parkland is free to walk in, with great views of the house and river, you could try leaving your car at Baslow or Calton Lees and walk up to the house instead.

Chatsworth Garden Centre Coffee Shop

Calton Lees, Beeley. Tel (01629) 734004
Grid ref: 259683
Open: Daily 10-5.30 (summer), 10-4.30 (winter)

Food: Breakfast baps till late morning, then afternoon hot meals from the blackboard can include dishes such as baked fish, liver and onions, tuna melt, and so on. All-day choice of jacket potatoes, sandwiches, filled Derbyshire oatcakes, as well as various slices, shortbread, cakes, scones, etc.

Drinks: Filter coffee, cappuccino and espresso, hot chocolate, and speciality teas, plus a range of cold drinks from the chill cabinet.

General: Located on the southern edge of Chatsworth Park, off the B6012 by the hamlet of Calton Lees, the coffee shop's opening times reflect that of the popular, 3-acre walled garden centre in which it is housed. The building itself is octagonal, with a high roof and several doors, a bit like a gigantic summer house. It's all self-service, with around 30 tables inside and a number on the terrace outside overlooking the plant sales area. No smoking or dogs inside. Fully wheelchair accessible, with dedicated disabled toilet facilities outside main entrance to garden centre. Walkers welcome.

CRESSBROOK- Derbyshire

This tiny, rather disparate community is tucked deep in a narrow fold of the River Wye, a mile north-west of Monsal Head (take the minor road down past the famous viaduct). D's Brew Stop is located behind the newly renovated Cressbrook Mill - follow the fenced walkway from the road. The mill, complete with bell tower, was built around 1815, and replaced an earlier cotton mill built by Richard Arkwright. Although now converted into private apartments its Georgian splendour can still be appreciated, while the Brew Stop itself is housed in the ground floor of the nearby apprentices' house, with its rather stern, castellated frontage. The riverside path continues beyond D's Brew Stop to reach an impressive tree lined

pool, flanked by towering cliffs, as the River Wye is channelled through the narrow limestone gap.

Dave Teare (centre) and helpers, D's Brew Stop

D's Brew Stop

Water-cum-Jolly, Cressbrook.
Tel (01298) 872103
Grid ref: 173727
Open: 10-5, weekends only.

Food: "This is not a café or a tea shop, but a loo-less brew stop," according to its owner Dave Teare. But although you are invited to eat your own food on the premises there are also cakes and confectionery for sale, plus a variety of ice creams.

Drinks: Served in small or large cups (all very reasonably priced): filter and instant coffee, English breakfast and speciality teas, malted milk, Barleycup, Bovril, plus a variety of drinks from the chill cabinet.

General: A unique establishment (in the very nicest sense!), D's Brew Stop opened in 1997 and is named after Dave Teare and his sons Danny and Dilwyn. Believed to be the first of its kind in the Peak District, it attracts cyclists, climbers, cavers and horse-riders, as well as large numbers of walkers from the nearby Monsal Trail, who revel in the relaxed atmosphere in which you are encouraged to enjoy your own sarnies over a mug of tea. There are a few seats inside, where various books,

Cressbrook – Cromford

maps and leaflets are on sale, otherwise it's a scattering of tables and benches in the peaceful yard outside, which in summer becomes a wonderful sun trap. Dogs on leads are welcome outside, where smoking is also permitted. Unfortunately there is no toilet, due to restrictions on Cressbrook's water processing system. The nearest loo is back at Monsal Head, so don't drink too much tea...

CROMFORD - Derbyshire

Located about two miles south of Matlock, off the A6, Cromford's place in the history books rests with the achievements of Sir Richard Arkwright, whose ground breaking cotton spinning mill located here on the River Derwent, helped set in motion the Industrial Revolution. Arkwright created the village of Cromford for his workforce, which remained in the family's ownership until the 1920s, and built the riverside Willersley Castle as his family home (see entry below). Today Cromford rumbles to the sound of traffic, especially quarry trucks and weekend motorbikes, but with a diverse range of tea rooms and coffee shops - plus a very pleasant towpath walk along the Cromford Canal - the area has much to recommend it once you get away from the main road.

Cromford Mill Restaurant

Cromford Mill, Mill Lane, Cromford.
Tel (01629) 823256
Grid ref: 297569
Open: Daily 9-5.
Food: With a vegetarian bias, the menu includes a range of fresh and interesting items all made on the premises. There are hot meals such as stilton and mushroom lasagne, celery and walnut roast, leek and cream cheese crumble, as well as filled rolls, home-made soups, jacket potatoes (at least 15 different fillings) and appetising cakes and puddings such as apricot and almond sponge, sticky date slice, and spicy apple sponge. Vegan options always available.

Drinks: Speciality teas include Assam, Darjeeling, Lady Grey, fennel, peppermint and rose hip, as well as Horlicks and a choice of fruit juices.

General: Small, light and welcoming tea room in the corner of the historic Cromford Mill, incorporating an exterior kiosk for take-aways. Plenty of outside seating, and ramps allow access inside for disabled visitors (ditto the toilet next door). No smoking inside, and dogs outside only (but free dog snacks and water bowls provided in summer). Altogether, feels smart and well run - tablecloths on every table, and also look out for the large number of local prints and paintings (all for sale) that adorn the wall. It's owned by the Arkwright Society, who are also planning to develop a new tea room just across the road in the warehouse at Cromford Wharf, at the end of the Cromford Canal. Large car park for mill and restaurant customers.

Masson Mill, Cromford

Derbyshire's little bit of world heritage

In December 2001 it was announced that the Derwent Valley had been awarded World Heritage Site status, putting it on par with the Taj Mahal and The Great Wall of China. Surely a mistake? Well, no, because the water-powered cotton spinning mill founded by Arkwright at Cromford in 1771 was the first of its kind anywhere in the world, and ushered in the new factory system that spread globally.

Today a 15-mile string of historic mills make up the Derwent Valley World Heritage Site - Masson and Cromford at this site, then Belper and Milford further downstream, followed by Darley Abbey and Derby Silk Mill. Each tell their own story of the unfolding Industrial Revolution, and no more so than at Cromford Mill, which was close to dereliction as recently as the

1970s but is now being renovated thanks to work by the Arkwright Society. There's an exhibition and daily guided tours of the mill, as well as the village, including separate tours for children; and as you would expect both Masson and Cromford Mills have jolly decent tea rooms. Sir Richard Arkwright's name may only be a dimly remembered detail from far off school history lessons for most people, but his legacy lives on. Early mills that used Arkwright's innovative technology at Pawtucket in New England, USA, and also at Cromford near Dusseldorf, Germany, have been restored and preserved as museums. World heritage indeed.

Derwent Restaurant

Masson Mills, Cromford. Tel (01629) 761522
www.massonmills.co.uk
Grid ref: 294573
Open: 10-5 Mon-Sat, 11-4.30 Sun and Bank Holidays.

Food: Changing menu of hot and cold food, snacks and light refreshments. Main meals include pies, fish, hot roast sandwiches, omelettes, and so on, and salad bar in summer. Children's choices; breakfast menu served 'till 11.30am (includes pancakes). Lighter items feature all-day paninis, scones and cakes, ice creams, etc. Senior citizens specials currently on Thursdays.

Drinks: Costa Coffee features latte, cappuccino, espresso and mocha; Earl Grey, iced tea, herbal infusions. Also licenced to sell wine and beer with dinner.

General: Large self-service restaurant (seating for 160) in Arkwright's impressive mill, built in brick on the banks of the River Derwent - access from A6. Masson were the oldest mills in the world in continuous production until finally ceasing in 1991, and now they're a popular visitor complex incorporating four floors of shops and craft outlets, plus the Working Textile Museum. The open-plan restaurant is light and airy, with attractive wrought iron tables spread out across a polished pine floor. It overlooks the river (although no outside seating), and ramps provide full wheelchair access - as they do to the nearby toilets. There's also a children's

area at the far side. No smoking, guide dogs only. Large pay and display car park, and charges refunded if food or drink (or shop items) purchased.

Reflections

Cromford Garden Centre, Derby Road, Cromford. Tel (01629) 824990
www.cromfordgardencentre.co.uk
Grid ref: 305565
Open: 9-4.30 Mon-Sat ('till 5 in summer), 9.30-4 on Sun, all year round.

Food: From hot main meals such as fish and chips, gammon, roast of the day, home-made curries, through to cream teas, pastries and cakes. Warm baguettes and jacket potatoes are also popular, and check out the specials board by the counter.

Drinks: Reflections is fully licensed, and there's a range of coffees and teas, plus milkshakes with added ice cream.

General: Refurbished a couple of years ago, this garden centre coffee shop is located half a mile south of Cromford on the A6. It is named after the mural painted on one of the walls by a local artist. The building is light and spacious, and in the summer tables are arranged on the patio outside, which also contains a giant chess board and pieces. The garden centre occupies terraces down to the Cromford Canal below, where there's a picnic area and nature/discovery trail for children. It also hosts regular talks and demonstrations by gardening experts on topics such as pruning, garden design, hanging baskets, etc. No smoking and no dogs in the coffee shop. Accessible for wheelchairs (plenty of ramps) but not so the toilets. Walkers welcome. Car park for customers.

Cromford

Scarthin Café

Scarthin, Cromford. Tel (01629) 823272
Grid ref: 295569
Open: 10-5.30 Mon-Sat, 12-5.30 Sun.

Food: Selection of home-made cakes and teabreads, including organic carrot cake, vegan chocolate cake, gluten-free polenta cake, plus apricot teacake and non dairy flapjack. Organic savouries include homity pie and nut loaf, and among their famous soups are parsnip and peanut, roasted peppers, and minestrone. Everything is prepared on the premises, and a children's menu is also available.

Drinks: Fair Trade coffee is at the top of the list, while the various teas number Jasmine, China Keemun, Darjeeling organic, Lapsang Souchong and Earl Grey organic. Other drinks include Barleycup and elderflower cordial.

General: This intimate and cosy café is situated on the first floor of the popular Scarthin Bookshop, overlooking the pond in the centre of the village. It's been a treasure trove for new and antiquarian books for 27 years, with shelves of books lining the walls, stairs and virtually every room in the building. A section near the door has a very good range of local and regional guides, booklets and reference works. The café welcomes book browsers, and also offers a varied and cultural magazine rack. Scarthin Books is the kind of place where you could happily lose yourself - and end up wondering where half the day had gone. Highly recommended. No dogs or smoking; toilets on top floor (including an old bath!). Limited parking.

Scarthin Books

Tors Café, Cromford

Tors Café

Derby Road, Cromford. Tel (01629) 825151
Grid ref: 296569
Open: 8.30-2 Mon-Fri only.

Food: Basic, uncomplicated and unfussy menu. Mainly centres on fry-ups, eggs/beans/cheese on toast, plus cobs and sandwiches with various fillings, at very reasonable prices. Quite probably the best value café food in the Peak District.

Drinks: Instant coffee, tea, hot chocolate and cans.

General: This peculiar hexagonal building, sitting by the busy junction on the A6 at Cromford, is so tiny it has just four tables. Previously a barbers shop, it resembles an old fashioned taxi shelter, and has been run as a café by the same couple for almost 30 years (and in the family for over 50). They describe it as "a happy little place, more like a pub atmosphere than a café", and over the years they've built up a loyal custom that ranges from local tradesmen, through to cycling groups and walkers (Chris Bonington has even been known to drop by.) Unshowy and unpretentious, it's a proper 'caff' in every sense of the word, with formica covered tables and rough benches. Don't expect to find tablecloths or doilies. Smoking and dogs allowed (no outside seating); public toilets across the road. Limited roadside parking off centre of Cromford, or pay and display by Cromford Wharf (5 mins walk).

> *"Take some more tea,' the March Hare said to Alice, very earnestly.*
> *'I've had nothing yet,' Alice replied in an offended tone, 'so I can't take more'.*
> *'You mean you can't take less,' said the Hatter, 'it's very easy to take more than nothing.'*

Willersley Castle, Cromford

Willersley Castle

Cromford (off Lea road, by Derwent bridge).
Tel (01629) 582270
Grid ref: 296573
Open: Daily 9.30-5.

Food: Aside from main meals at lunchtime, hot and cold snacks are served throughout the day. They include baked potatoes and toasted sandwiches, sandwiches and wholemeal hoagies or filled baps, scones and toasted teacakes, plus choices for children.

Drinks: Instant coffee, including decaffeinated, tea, hot chocolate and cold drinks.

General: Willerlsey Castle was built in the late 18th century for Richard Arkwright, the famous industrialist who has left his indelible mark on the whole of the Cromford area. It was eventually sold in 1925, and today is one of six properties across the country run by Christian Guild Holidays. Visitors are welcome, you don't need to be a resident to enjoy the facilities. Tea may be taken in one of the elegant lounges, or weather permitting on the seats outside. Wherever you sit you can marvel at the handsome, Grade II* listed building, with its high-ceilinged rooms and huge windows and fire places. It is set in 60 acres of landscaped grounds, through which runs the River Derwent. Although occasional conferences can make it busy, it's usually a very peaceful and calming place. No smoking; dogs outside only. Walkers welcome, and wheelchair access being developed during 2003. Car park for visitors.

DARLEY DALE- Derbyshire

A straggly, linear settlement in the Derwent valley north of Matlock, embracing a number of small communities such as Northwood, Churchtown and Two Dales.

Darley Dale Station

Darley Dale Station Tea Room

Off B5057 Winster road.
Tel (01629) 733476/580381
Grid ref: 274626
Open: 10.30-5 (summer), 10.30-4.30 (winter), on train operating weekends only.

Food: Various, reasonably priced hot and cold snacks, including filled cobs, soup, salads, pasties, toast, quiches and cakes. Afternoon and Cream teas, featuring fresh scones, are very popular. On certain Saturdays and Sundays hot meals are served as part of a proper set menu (includes Sunday roast), when the tea room becomes 'the Palatine Restaurant'. Booking ahead essential.

Drinks: Mugs or cups of tea (including Earl Grey, decaffeinated and herb) and coffee (filter and instant), plus Bovril, Horlicks, and various cold drinks.

General: Part of the original station buildings built in 1874, this small but very attractive period tea room is on the 'up' platform near the signal box and level crossing. The six tables include a couple of original and very comfortable carriage seats, plus there's an open fire and an array of interesting paintings and prints. There are further outside tables in the summer, plus a souvenir shop next door. No smoking or dogs inside. Ramp on to platform, where the toilets are wheelchair accessible. Free car park alongside the opposite platform, for Peak Rail visitors.

Darley Dale

Peak Rail

A preserved railway, Peak Rail operates steam rides between Rowsley and Matlock on selected weekends and weekdays throughout the year, with many special events, and in addition to their two station tea rooms there is often a small bar and buffet on board the actual trains. The short stretch of line between Rowsley and Matlock is part of the old Midland Railway's London to Manchester line, which closed in 1968. However, in the last few years there has been considerable debate about the possibility of reopening the entire line through the Peak District, via Bakewell and Buxton, and so reintroducing regular through services. Perhaps that's still some way off, and of course no one knows exactly how that would affect Peak Rail, so watch this space, as they say. To confirm Peak Rail's latest timetable call (01629) 580381 or visit their website at www.peakrail.co.uk.

Northwood Buffet, Darley Dale

Northwood Buffet

Rowsley South Station, off A6 south of Rowsley. Tel (01629) 580381

Grid ref: 263644

Open: 10.30-5 (summer), 10.30-4 (winter), train operating weekends and weekdays only.

Food: From sandwiches and soup through to sausage rolls and cakes. Hot offerings include chip butties, bacon and egg cobs, pasties, cheese/egg/spaghetti on toast and so on. You get the idea.

Drinks: Cup or mugs of tea and instant, filter or decaffeinated coffee (all available as take-away too), plus various cans, cartons and other cold drinks.

General: A long, low portacabin, the buffet sits next to the gift shop on the solitary platform, behind which is the vast car park (free to Peak Rail visitors). Bright, clean and functional, there are eight tables inside, and more outside in good weather. One small step for wheelchairs, but toilets on platform not wheelchair accessible. No smoking or dogs inside buffet.

> *"After a few months' acquaintance with European 'coffee' one's mind weakens, and his faith with it, and he begins to wonder if the rich beverage of home, with its clotted layer of yellow cream on top of it, is not a mere dream after all, and a thing which never existed."*
>
> Mark Twain 'A Tramp Abroad'

Tall Trees Coffee Shop and Restaurant

Forest Garden Centre, Oddford Lane, Two Dales. Tel (01629) 732932

Grid ref: 277627

Open: 9-4.30 Mon-Sat, 9-4 Sun.

Food: Freshly prepared on the (tiny!) premises, choose from lunchtime selections (12-2) such as home-made soup and quiche with salad, Sunday roast, Thai chicken curry, casseroles, and vegetarian options like roast peppers, tomato and goat's cheese tart. All-day options include cakes, tea cakes and scones, as well as flapjack, lemon cake, fudge brownies, date and oat slice, etc.

Drinks: Tea, filter coffee, fruit juices, and if eating the licence allows for wine and bottled beer.

General: Located at Forest Garden Centre off the A6 at the Chesterfield turning (between Darley Dale and Two Dales), this small but inviting place resembles a large octagonal summer house. Glass windows nearly all the way round means it's very light, and looking out over the rows of hebes, dwarf conifers and hardy perennials there's plenty to hold the attention. The restaurant is now 20 years old, and enjoys a good local custom. It's warm and comfortable inside, and although there's only nine tables (some of which may be reserved at lunchtime) the turnover is quite high and the friendly staff will try and secure you a table as soon as possible. Wheelchairs have to overcome just one small step, and the wheelchair accessible toilets are opposite. No smoking or dogs inside. Large, free car park for café and garden centre visitors.

EDALE- Derbyshire

This Dark Peak village north of Castleton, nestles at the foot of the Kinder Scout plateau. It is famous as the start/finish point for the Pennine Way, the challenging 250-mile long distance footpath that follows the high backbone of England into Scotland. The settlement consists of a number of different hamlets but all share a similar name: Barber Booth, Ollerbrook Booth, Upper Booth, Grindsbrook Booth - a 'booth' is an old name for a shepherd's or herdsman's shelter. Edale Cottage Café is next to the station, near the main pay-and-display car park, whereas Cooper's Café is at the far end of the lane at Grindsbrook Booth. On busy weekends it may be worth walking the ten minutes or so up the lane, past the church and National Park visitor centre, as parking spaces at the top are limited.

Cooper's Café, Edale

Cooper's Café

Grindsbrook Booth, Edale. Tel (01433) 670401
Grid ref: 123859
Open: Daily, 8.30-early evening (summer), 9-4/5 (winter).

Food: Hot and cold sandwiches, snacks, and wide range of hot meals from English and Veggie Breakfast through to burgers, pies, sausages and BLTs. 'Breakfast roll' includes Lorne sausage, bacon, egg and black pudding; plus there's cheese, beans and eggs on toast, as well as choices for children. Hot puddings feature jam, treacle and chocolate sponge with custard. Take-away sandwiches and snacks are served, and ice creams are on sale in the summer.

Drinks: Instant, filter and decaffeinated coffee, plus some more unusual teas - Lotus Green Tea, Twinings Exotic and peppermint.

General: Built three years ago to replace the original café housed in old railway carriages, this high-ceilinged building is clean and functional but largely devoid of character. The two spacious rooms (seating for 80, group bookings taken), both with tiled floors, make it ideal for walkers coming down from a day on Kinder. In summer the café will stay open as late as 8pm, depending on the weather. Self service; no dogs inside (two benches outside); smoking allowed in one room. Beware the TV blaring away in the corner. Wheelchair access at the rear with disabled toilet facilities. The café is located next to the post office and stores, opposite the Old Nags Head pub, where there is some very limited parking - otherwise leave your car at the pay-and-display car park at the beginning of the lane and walk up.

THE WORLD'S NO 1 DRINK
Coffee is the world's most popular beverage. A staggering 400 billion cups of it are consumed each year, making it a truly global commodity second only to oil in terms of revenue.

Edale – Edensor

The original Cooper's Café, Edale

The original Cooper's Café was constructed from two old railway carriages bolted together. It had great character and for decades was an institution amongst walkers. It was a great place to get warm, and enjoy a mug of tea, after a hard day on Kinder. It was a sad day indeed when those green doors closed for the last time.

Edale Cottage Café

Edale Cottage Café

Station Approach, Edale. Tel (01433) 670293
Grid ref: 124854
Open: Daily 9-5.30 Feb-end of Oct,
9-5 Nov-Jan (weekends only).

Food: Straightforward blackboard choice of sandwiches (eat in or take-away) or hot meals - pies and burgers, plus sausages, chips, bacon, eggs, etc (virtually any combination of these is possible, it seems). But no chips or burgers before noon. Also look out for the appetising cakes made by the owner's 77 year old mother: date and walnut is the most popular, plus Bakewell slice, ginger, chocolate and coconut. There are also scones and apple pie, confectionery and ice creams.

Drinks: Tea, coffee (filter or instant), hot chocolate, Bovril - all come in mugs or 'mega mugs' (1 pint); plus a range of cans and cartons of cold drinks.

General: An unpretentious little building near Edale Station run as a café for nearly 20 years, the single room interior sports seven solid pine tables and chairs. Underfoot are flag stones and an old carpet, testimony to the large numbers of walkers and cyclists who regularly drop by for refreshments. There's a small self-service hatch, a handwritten menu, and a few prints and posters on the walls, but this is more a place where you come for a plate of filling, hot food or a pint mug of tea, rather than a chance to admire the bone china. No smoking or dogs inside; two picnic benches out the front; customer toilets inside. Pay-and-display car park across the road near the Edale turning.

> *"The second day of a diet is always easier than the first. By the second day you're off it"* Jackie Gleason

EDENSOR- Derbyshire

This small village, pronounced 'Ensor', sits inside the Chatsworth Estate and is entirely owned by the Ducal family of Devonshire. The original settlement dates back to the Domesday Book, when it was called 'Edensoure', but in 1839 the 6th Duke of Devonshire decided to relocate most of the buildings - supposedly because they were too close to his house and spoilt the view! The story goes that when asked, by the architect, what design he wanted the new properties to take, he claimed he was too busy to choose, so he simply said "one of each". So if you look around the houses of Edensor today you will see a range of architectural styles - from Norman and Georgian to Swiss and Italian. Yes, really. The church was also replaced in the 19th century, and it includes various graves and memorials to the Devonshire family, including that of Kathleen Kennedy, sister of President John F. Kennedy, who married the 10th Duke's elder son.

Edensor Post Office and Tea Room

Edensor Post Office and Tea Room

Edensor. Tel (01246) 582283

Grid ref: 252699

Open: Daily 10-4 (summer),
10-4.30 (winter), closed Mon and Tues.

Food: Freshly prepared sandwiches, oatcakes, salads and ploughman's lunch, plus fruit pie and cream, cheese and biscuits, and of course popular cream teas. In fact the tea room is particularly noted for its scones, made from the base products (quality flour, local eggs) and baked in special tins. Also look out for their homemade soup, including leek and potato, and cream of tomato and courgette. "Soup is very emotive", according to proprietor Nigel Johnson. "Ours is fresh and dedicated, and as with the rest of our food as much as possible is sourced locally." Bradwells ice creams are also available for take away.

Scones, Edensor Tea Room

Drinks: Bewleys coffee, in cups and cafetieres, Yorkshire, Earl Grey, fruit teas, and hot chocolate 'whisked and served in a china beaker'.

General: One comfortable, carpeted room seating 34, off from the post office stores in the centre of the village (apparently it's been a post office and tea room since 1947). It's neat and a little twee, and although walkers are welcome they are requested to remove footwear. No smoking or dogs inside. Wheelchair accessible, as is the toilet outside. Car park for tea room visitors.

ELTON- Derbyshire

A quiet, rather out of the way village, south of Bakewell (off the B5056), which like Youlgrave and Winster and many other settlements in this White Peak area grew out of the lead mining industry. It's a popular location for walkers and cyclists, and the café (near the church and pub) is a popular stopping point on many weekend itineraries. Sadly the historic youth hostel will no longer feature on that list, as it was sold off by the YHA in 2002.

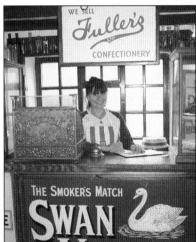

Jenny Hirst, Elton Café

Elton Café

Moor Lane, Elton. Tel (01629) 650217

Grid ref: 223609

Open: 10.30-5 weekends only.

Food: Freshly prepared soups (mostly vegetarian) and home-baked granary cobs, including locally sourced dry cured bacon. There's beans, eggs and chips or chip butties, salads and toasties, or homemade scones and cakes from the counter.

Drinks: Teas include Earl Grey, fruit and herbal infusions, pots or cups of filter coffee, milk shakes, hot chocolate and chilled fruit juices.

General: Popular with walkers and cycling groups (tiled floor throughout), this attractive guest house and weekend café near the village pub oozes character - from the antique cash till to the open fire in winter, the low-beamed ceiling and solid wooden tables and chairs to the walls crammed full of enamel advertising signs from yesteryear. The large, traditional cottage was once the village shop and post office, and although its small windows make it quite dark inside there's some outside seating in summer - where dogs and smokers are permitted. Table service. Wheelchair access to café and toilets. Parking on adjoining roads.

> *"Tea is water bewitched."*
> Chinese poet Lu-Wah

EYAM- Derbyshire

Eyam Tea Rooms

The popularity of this village, pronounced 'Eem', rests squarely, and you might think a little uncomfortably, on its role during the plague 300 years ago. A tailor from London unwittingly introduced the plague to the village from a damp parcel of cloth. As it began to take hold the community went into a self-imposed quarantine to prevent the disease from spreading. Around 350 villagers died in this selfless act, and there are numerous signs and notices recording when and where the unfortunate men, women and children perished. In the high season visitors come by the coachload to be appalled, and

maybe buy a souvenir or two. The Rookery tea room, in particular, enters into the spirit of things with their imaginatively-named 'Plague Pie', and despite some initial misgivings the author (publisher and artist too) can report that it was in fact delicious and has had no discernible side effects so far. In addition to the two tea rooms, the Peak Pantry on the Square (at the eastern end of the village, near the pub) serves a range of tasty savouries, and cakes, either to take away or to be enjoyed on the picnic benches outside. Teas, coffees and cold drinks are also available.

David Joyce, Eyam Tea Rooms

Eyam Tea Rooms

The Square, Eyam. Tel (01433) 631274
Grid ref: 221765
Open: Daily 10-5 (summer), 10-4/4.30 (winter)
Food: Full range of choices, from sandwiches, pork pie platter and salads through to hot meals such as Sunday roast, home-made steak pie, gammon and omelettes (see specials board). There's soup, paninis and 'toasted treats', plus cakes and sweets. Look out for the set Eyam Cream Tea, Fruitcake Tea and 'Pot-pourri of fruit'.

Drinks: Eyam Tea Rooms has its own blend of coffee prepared by Pollards (Blue Mountain Costa Rica), and filter coffee re-fills are free. There's also espresso, mocha, cappuccino and decaffeinated, while the teas range from English breakfast, Assam, Darjeeling and Earl Grey through to assorted herbal and fruit infusions. Hot chocolate served in a tall glass. There are also milk shakes (strawberry, lime, chocolate, banana, raspberry) made with ice cream; and the premises are also licenced.

General: Overlooking Eyam's main square, the surprisingly large interior (over a dozen tables) has a homely, chintzy feel, with a patterned carpet, wallpaper and decorative plates around the walls. Look out for the range of prints and paintings (for sale) by local artists. Toilets and outside seating (no smoking inside). Walkers and groups welcome, and well-behaved dogs also allowed inside. Dating from the 17th century, the building once formed part of the Bold Rodney Inn, which closed in 1901. The name lives on in the Bold Rodney Bistro, when the lights are lowered and the tables re-arranged as the long room turns into an evening restaurant (7-9, Thurs-Sat) with an accompanying menu and wine list. Both tea room and bistro are waitress service. To book a table at the bistro call 01433 631730. Parking along adjoining streets, or in main visitor car park at far end of village.

Sonia Postance, The Rookery, Eyam

The Rookery

Main Road, Eyam. Tel (01433) 639666
Grid ref: 215765
Open: Daily 10-5 or later (summer), 10.30-4.30 (winter)

Food: An imaginative and quality menu, ranging from light snacks like brie and grape baguettes and Hartington stilton and marmalade jacket potatoes through to home-made casseroles, soups, roast

Sunday lunch, etc. Look out for the Sage Derby cheese pie, and the so-called 'Plague Pie' filled with currants. There's always a specials board and vegetarian options, with bakes and sweets like lemon meringue and gateaux, plus traditional cream teas. Everything is home-made - they bake their own scones and cakes, even their own baguettes.

Drinks: Licenced (choice of wines), with soft drinks including Buxton mineral water and milk shakes. Teas include Darjeeling, Assam, Earl Grey and organic decaffeinated, while speciality coffee includes cappuccino and espresso - all are from Northern Tea Merchants in Chesterfield.

General: Occupying the first floor (above their own gift and antiques shop), this is a tastefully decorated and elegant tea room mixing handsome wooden tables and chairs with walls full of interesting old prints and paintings (all for sale). There's a small outside terrace at the back, and in summer a couple of tables and chairs are placed back from the pavement by the front door downstairs (where the toilet is also situated). Walkers, children and "small dogs" are welcome; smoking outside only. Friendly table service. Highly commended in Tea Room/Coffee House of the Year awards 2003. Limited parking on street, or pay-and-display car park nearby.

W.I. Country Markets

When it comes to producing high quality home-made jams, pickles, cakes and pies, the Women's Institute is in a class of its own. Forget the pearls and blue rinses, and think instead of three-fruit marmalade, lemon curd, apricot jam, sponge cakes, apple pie... If that has got your mouth watering then go along to the W.I. Country Markets at Bakewell (Town Hall, every Sat morning), Hope Valley (Methodist Schoolrooms, Fri mornings) and Matlock (Imperial Rooms, every Fri morning). They even operate a parcel scheme so you can send a batch of goodies to a friend, have it delivered to your home or holiday cottage, and so on. See www.wimarkets.co.uk or call 0118 939 4646 for more details.

Grindleford – Hartington

GRINDLEFORD- Derbyshire

The café is located by Grindleford Station, a mile north east of the village, off the B6521 (the location is shown as Nether or Upper Padley on some maps).

Station Café, Grindleford

Grindleford Station Café

Station Approach, Grindleford. Tel (01433) 631001

Grid ref: 252787

Open: Daily 8.30-5 (summer), 8.30-4 (winter)

Food: No-nonsense blackboard menu ranging from cooked breakfast (including vegetarian), filled Yorkshire puddings, burgers, pasties, pies and omelettes through to lighter 'toasted meals' such as beans, eggs, sardines, sausages. Beware - the chip butties are substantial. Also: teacakes and toast, hot sweets (spotted dick, treacle sponge, chocolate sponge and custard) and children's menu. Confectionery and ice cream scoops also available.

```
Tea ½ Pint 80 p
Tea Pint £ 1-30
Coffee ½ Pint 95p
Coffee Pint £1-50
Black Coffee ½ Pint 80p
Black Coffee Pint £1.25
```

Drinks: Instant tea and coffee in half or pint mugs, plus hot chocolate, Bovril, Horlicks. The premises is also licenced (beer, wine, spirits), and the menu includes milky coffee with rum/whisky/brandy.

General: Housed in the former station building by the entrance to Totley tunnel, this long-established café is popular with walkers and climbers, who enjoy the large, no frills portions and all-round bustle. The two main rooms are fairly basic with bare floors and wooden slatted walls, but retain the character of the building with original station benches, light fittings, and so on. The open fire is welcome in winter, but in summer the huge array of outside tables (some covered) are very popular. Food is dispensed in a self-service, canteen style. The café is fully accessible for wheelchairs; smoking is permitted in one room; but dogs and mobile phones are banned! In fact there are quite a few rules, sorry 'requests' to observe here - you have been warned! There are books and newspapers for sale at the counter, and also look out for the café's own spring water that is bottled from a natural spring at the back of the building. Free parking on Station approach.

HARTINGTON- Derbyshire

On seemingly every visitor's itinerary, Hartington has a range of shops, pubs and cafes around a main square, the central part of which is often a busy car park. But a key attraction is, of course, the surrounding countryside, and most notably the path into Dove Dale to the south, with its beautiful river winding between soaring limestone cliffs. However, there are some fine period buildings in and around the village, especially the 17th century Hartington Hall, which after a recent £1m refit is now a handsome and deservedly popular youth hostel. There is also a working creamery at Hartington, and the Old Cheese Shop off the market place sells a range of locally-made cheeses, including the famous Hartington Stilton, Dovedale Blue and Buxton Blue. For more information see www.hartingtoncheese.com

> *The naming of teas is a difficult matter.*
> *It isn't just one of your everyday games-*
> *Some might think you as mad as a hatter*
> *Should you tell them each goes by several names.*
> *For starters each tea in this world must belong*
> *To the families Black or Green or Oolong;*
> *Then look more closely as these family trees-*
> *Some include Indians along with Chinese.*
>
> T.S. Eliot The Naming of Cats

Beresford Tea Rooms

Beresford Tea Rooms

Market Place, Hartington. Tel (01298) 84418
Grid ref: 128604
Open: Daily 10.30-5 (summer),
10.30-3 (winter)

Food: Hot meals and snacks tailored for the seasons, so the likes of hot pot in winter and quiche and salad in summer. Regular menu includes all-day breakfast, ciabattas, smoked trout, ploughman's, toasties and open sandwiches, plus home-made cakes and desserts like Bakewell tart and rhubarb crumble. Specials include Mexican chilli oatcakes, and home-baked biscuits. Bradwells ice cream sold by the scoop.

Drinks: Tea (English Breakfast, Earl Grey, Assam, Darjeeling, herbal and fruit infusions), filter coffee, milk shakes, hot chocolate, and the usual range of cold drinks.

General: On the main square next to the Devonshire Arms, the small and compact Beresford Tea Rooms now incorporates the village post office, and with a gift shop at the front it can get decidedly crowded at peak times. The half a dozen tables are clustered around the side and back, surrounded by wooden chairs. Prints of local scenes decorate the walls. The café is popular with walkers and cyclists. The toilet is accessible for wheelchairs. There's no outside seating, and dogs are not allowed inside. No smoking. Free parking in village centre, but it can be limited at busy periods.

> *"Never eat more than you can lift."*
> Miss Piggy, 'The Muppet Show'

Corner House Tea Rooms, Hartington

Corner House Tea Rooms

Market Place, Hartington. Tel (01298) 84365
Grid ref: 128604
Open: 11-5 Sat-Wed (summer),
11-4 weekends only (winter).

Food: 'All day snacks' such as toast, teacakes, toasted sandwiches and jacket potatoes, while 'fancies' include scones with jam, cream, etc. There are also three set cream teas. The range of hot meals from the lunchtime menu (12-2.30) includes cottage pie, stilton and vegetable crumble, fish, etc - and see specials board. There is also a range of cakes and sweets.

Drinks: Filter coffee, speciality teas (Assam, Darjeeling, Earl Grey) and a range of cold drinks.

General: Comprising a smart, neat single room, originally part of a licenced guest house (hence the elaborate wooden framed bar area), it's fully carpeted with ordered pine tables. There's always plenty of staff on duty (table service), and look out in particular for the collection of eccentric teapots on the picture rail, and the cuttings and pictures on the walls depicting the owners' fundraising endeavours, on behalf of the Guide Dogs for the Blind. Walkers welcome, but please remove muddy boots. Front steps and toilet out the back make wheelchair access awkward. No smoking or dogs. Free parking nearby, but busy at peak times.

Peak District Beer

A remote farmhouse a couple of miles south of Hartington is the base for Whim Brewery, one of only two breweries still operating in the Peak District. Established in 1993 and not open to the public, their range of fine beers, including Hartington Bitter and IPA, Arbor Light and Magic Mushroom, can be sampled in a few local pubs, such as the Charles Cotton Hotel in Hartington.

To the south, approaching Ashbourne on the A515 at Fenny Bentley, Leatherbritches Brewery is part of the Bentley Brook Inn, and their various beers and porters can be sampled on the premises. In addition to draught, Leatherbritches also bottles its own beer, so that you can take away your very own Bespoke or Hairy Helmet for enjoyment elsewhere. Tours of the tiny brewery are possible by prior arrangement, and there are even occasional beer festivals - which the author has been known to attend purely for the purposes of literary research, of course. See 'The Peak District Pub Guide' by Andrew McCloy (Johnson Publishing, 2002).

HASSOP- Derbyshire

Country Bookshop is in fact located midway between Bakewell and Hassop on the B6001, by the roundabout with the A6020.

Whistlestop Café

Country Bookshop, Hassop Station, Hassop.
Tel (01629) 813444
www.countrybookshop.co.uk
Grid ref: 217706
Open: Daily 10-4.30.

Food: Small but appetising range of snacks, including filled rolls, pastries and slices, home-made soups, salad bar, and always vegetarian and vegan options. Cakes include orange and lemon, spiced apple, and carrot cake. Bradwell's traditional dairy ice cream is also on sale.

Drinks: Fair Trade teas and coffees, including decaffeinated and speciality teas (fruit and herbal), plus traditional lemonade.

General: Developed a couple of years ago for customers browsing the popular bookshop, the café has developed into a regular stop for walkers and cyclists enjoying the Monsal Trail. The bookshop uses the old station building, so of course the trail passes right by. There's limited seating, including some tables among the actual shelves on the shop floor, but since there's also outside seating in the summer, you can usually get a place (and simply browse in the meantime). Wheelchair access to the shop and café, but not at present to the toilets. No smoking and no dogs inside. Large free car park.

HATHERSAGE- Derbyshire

In the churchyard of St Michael and All Angels, off the main street, is an extralong grave supposedly the last resting place of Little John. Robin Hood connections abound in the Peak District, with Robin Hood's Cross near Bradwell, Robin Hood's Stride near Birchover and Robin Hood's Cave, high above Hathersage on Stanage Edge. The linear, gritstone outcrops of Stanage form an eye-catching natural barrier, and have long been a mecca for climbers. Indeed, more and more outdoor and equipment stores are springing up in Hathersage to cater for the ever-expanding leisure market. The village was once noted more for its needle and pin-making industry, and also for its millstones. These heavy stone discs were used in pairs for grinding, and were quarried from the surrounding gritstone edges. The millstone has become the symbol of the Peak District National Park.

Merlyn, Cintras Restaurant and Tea Rooms, Hathersage

Cintras Restaurant and Tea Rooms

Main Street, Hathersage. Tel (01433) 651825
Grid ref: 230815
Open: Daily 8.30-6/6.30 (summer), 9.30-4.30 (winter).

Food: Wide-ranging menu, from baguettes and salads through to hot meals, including breakfasts, pies, fish and chips. There are also toasties, cream teas, croissants, muffins and tea cakes. House specialities include home-made steak pie, and Greek feta salad.

Drinks: Pots of tea, including herbal infusions, filter coffee (with free top-ups) and milk shakes. But also check out the popular and well-prepared speciality coffees: espresso, cappuccino, latte, mocha and Americano. The café and restaurant is fully licenced, and bottled lager, beer and wine is available with meals.

General: Situated near the George Hotel at the bottom of the main road, Cintras has a small, neat downstairs room, with lace table cloths, willow-patterned china and gentle piped music. Upstairs it's also table service, but from Spring 2003 this smart, larger room doubles up as an attractive evening restaurant (seating 36). At the back there is a popular tea garden with seating for up to 60. The downstairs area is wheelchair accessible, including the toilets. Walkers very welcome; dogs in the garden only. Limited parking available on main road by shops, or pay and display car park off Oddfellows Road.

Country Fayre Tea Room, Hathersage

Country Fayre Tea Room

Hathersage Craft Shop, Main Street, Hathersage. Tel (01433) 650858
Grid ref: 231815
Open: Varies from 10.30/11-5/6, daily in summer and winter weekends ('till 4/5), with occasional opening on winter weekday afternoons (ring ahead to check first).

Food: Well-known for authentic home baking, with a specialist dessert menu that may include the likes of apple and almond flan, crumbles with real fruit, baked egg custard, chocolate flan, and plain and iced Bakewell puddings. There are also home-made flans and scones, and the main menu features sandwiches, toasties, oatcakes (hot savoury with a variety of cheese fillings), salads, pasties and ploughman's. Or you can opt for the set Country Fayre Afternoon Tea or Cream Tea.

Drinks: Ground coffee in cups or mugs, hot chocolate, Earl Grey, Darjeeling, Assam and fruit/herbal teas.

General: A small but homely first floor tea room, situated above a craft shop (open daily) opposite the garage on the main street in Hathersage. There are seven tables, arranged around pine booths, with plenty of paintings and prints adorning the walls and gentle background music. Friendly table service. Locally-made Bradwell's ice cream is available downstairs. No dogs or smoking. There are no toilets inside, but the public toilets are nearby. Limited parking on main road, or pay and display off Oddfellows Road.

Oddfellows Pool Café and Tea Room

Oddfellows Road, Hathersage.
Tel (01433) 651159.
Grid ref: 233814
Open: Daily 10-6 (summer) - and later when pool is open, 10-4/5 (winter).

Food: Morning brunch 'till noon features English breakfast, toast, etc, and good value 'From the griddle' options include hot sandwiches, pies, jacket potatoes and toasties. Also soups and roll, and salad platters. 2-course special on Fridays, roast dinner on Sundays, and a take-away fish and chips service. The 'Hikers' Hash', in a

Hathersage – Hope

Yorkshire Pudding, is especially popular with hungry outdoor types. In addition, there are scones, sandwiches, cream teas, and home baked cakes (some made by the local W.I.) featuring lemon yoghurt, coffee, cherry and sultana, etc. The lengthy children's menu is also more imaginative than most.

Drinks: Tea by the pot, including speciality teas and herbal infusions, cafetières of fresh coffee, hot chocolate, milk shakes, and a range of cold drinks.

General: The café is situated on a back street beyond the tennis courts, and part of the outdoor swimming pool area. It comprises one light, open main room with nine glass-topped tables. This is no twee tea room, rather a popular local café that also attracts outdoor groups who enjoy the well-priced portions. In summer it's busy with pool-goers into the early evenings. The Hathersage outdoor lido (heated) is a gem, and one of the very few left of its kind. There's no better way to round off a swimming session, than to enjoy a drink, or snack, on the café's newly refurbished patio. Dogs and smokers are allowed outside. Although a ramp allows wheelchair access to the café, the inside toilets are not yet wheelchair accessible. Limited parking outside, but a large pay and display car park opposite.

HOPE - Derbyshire

Located midway between Hathersage and Castleton, at the turn for the Edale valley, the village of Hope is surrounded by angular peaks and ridges, most notably Lose Hill and Win Hill. According to popular legend, this was the scene of a great battle back in the Dark Ages, as the kings of Wessex and Northumbria and their respective armies faced each other from opposing hilltops. King Edwin and his Northumbrian forces triumphed on the day, clinching the bloody encounter by rolling a shower of boulders down upon the hapless warriors from Wessex, so that Edwin's hill became known as Win Hill and... you've guessed it. Of course, there's little direct evidence that any of this actually took place, but why let hard facts get in the way of a good story? (*Note from the boring editor - Win may be a corruption of 'whin' - a north country word for gorse or furze*). The two cafés are located on the main street by the shops, nearly opposite the church. Also check out the Hope Chest, a superior deli that does tasty take-away fare.

Fair Trade - for all

An initiative that is quickly spreading nationwide, Fair Trade aims to ensure that producers of what we eat, drink or buy get a fair deal. Coffee-growers and tea-pickers in the Developing World generally earn a pittance, since the big firms continue to cream off all the profits. In fact, world coffee prices are at a 30-year low, but of course the prices in our shops don't reflect that! Fair Trade tea and coffee is already well-known and very popular, but there are in fact over 100 Fair Trade brands that include chocolate, banana juice, sugar and honey - all of them carry the distinctive logo. In the Peak District you can find Fair Trade tea and coffee at amongst other places Scarthin Books Café in Cromford and Good for You! in Matlock, and during Spring 2003 a campaign was mounted to turn the Hope Valley into Britain's first 'Fair Trade valley'. For more information see www.fairtrade.org.uk

Courtyard Café

The Courtyard, 8 Castleton Road, Hope.
Tel (01433) 623360
Grid ref: 173836
Open: Daily 9.30-5 (summer), 10-4 (winter)
Food: Standard menu ranges from scrambled egg and poached eggs through to tea cakes and scones, as well as sandwiches, salads and jacket potatoes. The specials board can include the likes of spinach and ricotta cannelloni, leek and mushroom crumble, plus the perennial favourite scrambled egg and smoked salmon on toast. Also look out for the list of hot desserts.
Drinks: Cafetières of coffee, pots of fresh tea including Earl Grey and herbal/fruit

infusions, and milkshakes and other cold drinks.

General: Bright, two-roomed café behind Hope's parade of shops. The yellow-stencilled walls, pine furniture, and tiled floor give it a light, modern feel, especially as the back room is a glass-roofed conservatory. Pictures from the gallery, across the courtyard, hang on the walls. In winter a stove is in use. At the back there's a large area of outside seating. Dogs allowed inside, but smoking is restricted to the outside tables. The café and toilets (across the back yard) are wheelchair accessible.

Home-baking at the Woodbine Café, Hope

Woodbine Café

18 Castleton Road, Hope. Tel (01433) 621407
Grid ref: 173836
Open: Daily 9-5 (summer), 9-4 (winter),
8.30-4 at weekends.

Food: The majority of the food is prepared fresh on the premises, including giant Yorkshire puddings filled with homemade casserole, chilli or curry, plus huge pasties, scones, cakes and desserts including apple pie. There's also soups and hot sandwiches, jacket potatoes, and 'light lunches' featuring risotto, lasagne, ploughman's, and tuna bake. Gluten-free, vegetarian and vegan options are also available. The locally-made Bradwells ice cream is sold in scoops by the front door.

Drinks: Filter coffee, cappuccino, latte, milk shakes made with ice cream, hot chocolate with marshmallows or cream, Horlicks, and Twinings speciality teas.

General: A small and cosy café, the ear-

liest part of the building dates from the 17th century and was once a pub called the Blacksmiths Arms. Beyond the front counter, which does a popular take-away service, there are a handful of wooden benches in front of a grand fireplace (lit in winter). The stone flagged floor and whitewashed walls give it a nice period feel, and out the back there's more seating in the tea garden. Well-frequented by walkers and campers, who often come here for a cooked breakfast, there are books and maps for sale, and it can get a little cramped when busy (order food and drink at counter). No smoking or dogs inside. The café is accessible for wheelchairs, but not the toilets at the rear.

> *"Qu'ils mangent de la brioche!"* ("*Let them eat cake!*") Queen Marie-Antoinette

ILAM- Derbyshire

This small estate village, standing on the confluence of the Rivers Dove and Manifold, was remodelled in the 19th century by the shipping magnate Jesse Watts-Russell, whose love of mock-Gothic design extended to the hall and church. One of the reasons for the incongruous Alpine style of some of the cottages is that the view of the soaring, pointed peaks above Dove Dale (such as Thorpe Cloud and Bunster Hill) reminded him of the Alps. Just as well he didn't holiday in Blackpool. Ilam Hall was partially demolished in the 1930s, and the dark, stern remainder is now a youth hostel. The National Trust visitor centre has more details on Ilam's history.

View from Ilam Tea Rooms

Ilam Hall Tea Room

Ilam Hall. Tel (01335) 350245
Grid ref: 132506
Open: 11-5 Fri-Tues (summer),
11-4 weekends only (winter)

Food: Blackboard menu includes soup, cream teas, cakes, sandwiches, plus daily hot meals from main counter. Everything is made fresh in the kitchens, and among the regular meals are the 'Ramblers' Lunch', potato cakes, and Staffordshire oatcakes filled with the likes of Hartington stilton and onion, Red Leicester and chutney or tomato, and so on. Plenty of vegetarian choices, in particular. They also do children's lunchboxes (or kids can also have half portions, at half the price of main meals).

Drinks: Range of speciality teas and filter coffee, plus the usual choice of cold drinks.

General: Self-service tea room on the National Trust's popular estate near the foot of Dove Dale. The long and spacious building has been tastefully renovated, with exposed beams and a high roof, and there are rows of pine tables that in summer spill out on to the attractive grass terrace. No wheelchair access, but food and drink will be brought down to the nearby courtyard during the summer on request. Prints and paintings by local artists adorn the walls, and there are pleasant views out across the Manifold Valley from the windows at the southern end of the building. No smoking or dogs in the tea room. Toilets are by the National Trust shop and information centre in the courtyard below, and the pay and display car park is free to National Trust members. There is no charge to enter Ilam Park.

LONGNOR - Staffordshire

Located high on a ridge between the Upper Dove and Manifold, the attractive village of Longnor sits just inside Staffordshire (someone please tell the Post Office). The cobbled main square was once an important stopping and trading point for wagons moving between the Potteries and the Cheshire plain, to towns and cities such as Sheffield and Nottingham. It is still the focus for the community, and is surrounded by three pubs and two cafés. Dominating the square is the old market hall, now a craft centre and coffee shop, and above the main door is the original list of dues payable by stallholders and buyers.

Longnor Craft Centre and Coffee Shop, Longnor

Longnor Craft Centre and Coffee Shop

Market Place, Longnor. Tel (01298) 83587
www.longnorcrafts.co.uk
Grid ref: 088649
Open: Daily 10-5 (mid Feb-Dec),
10-5 Fri-Sun only (Jan-mid Feb)

Food: Light lunches, rather than main meals, such as home-made soups (prepared on the premises) - carrot and coriander, pea and ham, chunky farmhouse vegetable - quiche and salad, ploughman's lunch and hot savoury oatcakes (cheese with apple, cheese with mushroom, cheese with spring onion). There are home-baked cakes, including carrot cake, date and walnut, and farmhouse fruit cake (with low fat options); plus scones, toasted teacakes, and so on.

Drinks: Filter coffee, including decaffeinated, Breakfast, Earl Grey, fruit and herbal infusions (groups are treated to the giant 'Big Bertha' teapot!), and a range of cold drinks.

General: The craft centre and coffee shop is housed in the former market hall, built in the 18th century and overlooking Longnor's main square. The coffee shop is at one end of the ground floor, and (with a special ramp) is accessible for wheelchair visitors. The craft centre is run by Fox

Country Furniture; it has an elegant gallery with art exhibitions throughout the year, and showcases a range of high-quality local arts and crafts. From pottery to jewellery, wood-turned bowls to tables, all the items are for sale. "We are not just another gift shop!" says owner Peter Fox. It's one of the few coffee shops in the Peak where you can sit at quality, hand-made wooden tables and chairs. No smoking or dogs inside. A few benches outside at the front. Toilets on ground floor. Walkers and cyclists welcome. Free parking on the market place.

Frankly Scarlett Café

Bank House, Market Place, Longnor.
Tel (01298) 83659
Grid ref: 088649
Open: Thurs-Fri 10-4 (summer only),
9-5 at weekends.

Food: Sandwiches and light snacks made to order, including cakes baked on premises. The café is especially noted for all-day breakfasts: 'The Longnor Belly Buster' comprises sausages, bacon, egg, oatcake, black pudding and beans, plus there's the Longnor Smiler and Longnor Lean-un, and a smaller kids' version. There are also oatcake wraps, featuring fillings such as bacon and stilton, apricot and brie and onion, spinach and ricotta.

Drinks: Tea and instant coffee (free refills), hot chocolate and a range of cold drinks.

General: Named after a line in the film 'Gone With the Wind', this attractive corner café overlooking the main square was previously a gift shop. Look out for the numerous model and toy hens dotted around the room! The single room has four tables, plus a fifth outside during the summer. Its high ceiling, polished wooden floor and elegant shop windows give it an airy and inviting feel. Table service. The café has won an environment quality award from the Peak National Park, as it strives to use only locally-sourced food - the meat is from local, naturally reared animals, free from growth hormones, and the eggs are of course free range. Public toilets across the road; dogs welcome. No smoking inside. Parking in the old, cobbled market place.

Coffee choices demystified

Americano:
Espresso diluted with hot water.
Amaretto:
Latte with almond syrup.
Cappuccino:
Espresso topped with foamed milk, its name coming from the pale brown robes worn by Capuchin monks.
Con Panna:
Espresso topped by whipped cream.
Creme:
Espresso with heavy cream.
Espresso:
Shot of strong black coffee prepared by forcing or 'pressing' steam at very high pressure through finely ground, dark roast coffee beans, extracting all the flavour possible.
Filter Coffee:
Served in a cafetière, which has an in-built filter to separate the ground coffee from hot water.
Freddo:
Chilled espresso in a glass.
Au Lait:
Coffee and boiled milk.
Latte:
Espresso with steamed milk, topped by foamed milk.
Con Leche:
Espresso with steamed milk.
Macchiatto:
Espresso 'marked' with a little foamed milk ('macchiatto' means 'marked').
Mocha:
Latte with chocolate, and various preparations such as whipped cream and cocoa powder.
Ristretto:
Short concentrated shot of coffee.

LONGSHAW - Derbyshire

The National Trust's Longshaw Estate covers 1,600 acres of open moorland and wooded hillside of the Derwent Valley between Grindleford and Hathersage. It is in fact only ten miles away from the centre of Sheffield. Longshaw Lodge, near the visitor centre and now private, was built in 1827 as a shooting lodge for the Duke of

Longshaw

Rutland. Immediately below is Longshaw Meadow, where the country's longest running sheepdog trials are held every September. They began in 1898, apparently to settle an argument between local farmers and shepherds over who had the best sheepdog. The estate is criss-crossed with scenic paths and tracks, and one of the loveliest is alongside Burbage Brook that descends through the tumbling, tree-covered hillside of Padley Gorge.

Longshaw Visitor Centre

Longshaw Visitor Centre

Longshaw Estate. Tel (01433) 631708
Grid ref: 265798
Open: Daily 10.30-5 Jun-end Sept, Nov-end March weekends only, Apr-May Wed-Sun only.
Food: Choice of fresh cakes and slices, plus imaginative blackboard selections all freshly made on the premises, including award winning fish-shaped smoked trout scones, served with a salad and horseradish dip. Also spinach and mushroom pie (featuring goats cheese in a filo pastry wrap), plus Derbyshire ham salad, homity pie, macaroni cheese, flans and filled oatcakes. Children's menu available.
Drinks: Filter and decaffeinated coffee, hot chocolate, speciality teas such as Earl Grey, peppermint and rose hip infusions, plus a range of cold drinks.
General: This long, low building next to Longshaw Lodge is part National Trust visitor centre and gift shop, and part self-service café - apparently teas and refreshments have been served here since 1927. It's a popular spot for walkers and families enjoying the paths, woodland and open moorland of this famous Dark Peak estate, and in summer people spill out out of the café on to the tables and chairs outside. Inside, the ten or so tables are a little squashed (and it really can get crowded at weekends), but nevertheless it's a warm and cosy interior, with plenty of wall displays. Fairly wheelchair accessible (one slight step), outside toilets with disabled facilities, open all the time. No smoking or dogs inside. Pay-and-display car park nearby (free for National Trust members).

Food and drink of the Peak District

In addition to the farmers markets and WI Country markets, there are specialist producers and outlets across the Peak District that make a tea shop tour through the dales even more attractive. For instance, the Bentley Brook Inn at Fenny Bentley, near Ashbourne, is the home of Leatherbritches Brewery, which produces a fine range of quality cask ales and bottled conditioned beers. Peak Feast at Youlgrave produce ready-made meals, organic cakes and vegetarian and vegan savouries (some available via Hollands butchers in the village), and you can pick your own strawberries and raspberries at the Promised Land Fruit Farm above Darley Dale. The Old Cheese Shop at Hartington sells amongst others the locally-made Stilton, Buxton Blue and Dovedale Blue; while Caudwell's Mill on the River Wye produces a range of specialist flours (see entry under 'Rowsley'). There are numerous farms supplying free range and organic eggs, and local meat suppliers include Watsons in the Hope Valley, New Close at Over Haddon through to Buxton Shepherd's Lamb at Hollinsclough and Rare Breeds Meats at Riddings Park Farm near Ashbourne. For an up to date list, see www.peakdistrictfoods.co.uk. Well worth visiting is The Original Farmers Market Shop in Bakewell, which stocks only food and drink produced in and around the Peak District. There are further opportunities to buy local produce at the monthly Farmers Markets in Ashbourne(third Sat of the month), Bakewell (last Sat) and Buxton (second Sat).

MATLOCK - Derbyshire

There's a diverse range of cafés and coffee rooms to be found in Matlock, a busy town that sits astride the River Derwent. It is more of a working town than Bakewell, and although outside the National Park, is a good base for exploring the Peak District. Its modern development began around 150 years ago, when the health-giving thermal springs of Matlock Bath became popular. At one time there were as many as 30 local 'hydros', that offered restorative water treatments and cures. One of the best known was John Smedley's Hydro, an imposing building high on the hillside overlooking the town, and after closing in 1955 it later became the offices of Derbyshire County Council. The popularity of the various hydros and baths was ultimately short-lived, but in a timely turning of the circle the district council has recently approved plans for a new public leisure complex in Matlock, due to open in 2004/5, and which will hopefully include a brand new swimming pool. It seems water still has its attraction, after all.

Cine Café, Matlock

Cine Café

43 Bakewell Road, Matlock.
Tel (01629) 56666
www.matlockmotorcycles.co.uk
Grid ref: 294605
Open: 9-5 (Mon-Sat), 10-5 (Sun), last hot food orders at 4pm.

Food: Hot food counter serves dishes such as lasagne, pies, Sunday roast (pork and beef), curry, soup, most of which is freshly prepared on the premises. The all-day breakfast is particularly popular. But there's also a range of sandwiches, toasted tea cakes, etc, and desserts such as crumble, meringue, gateaux, etc.

Drinks: Latte, mocha, cappuccino and regular filter coffee available, plus tea (jug of fresh milk provided on counter), hot chocolate and chilled drinks.

General: Part of Matlock Motorcycle Centre, 1/4 mile south of Matlock town centre on the A6, the self-service Cine Café is large (30 tables) and split-level, even incorporating a balcony. The high ceiling design echoes the chequered flag theme, and the modernistic steel and pine furniture is surrounded by large mirrors. Dominating everything is a huge video screen, showing endless clips of motorbike races, stunts, music videos, etc. There are new and classic bikes dotted around the café, and you have to walk through the extensive showroom to get to the cafe, BUT leathers and crash helmets are not compulsory! There are plenty of non-biking customers, and a ramp makes the café and toilets fully accessible for wheelchair users. Smoking discouraged but not banned. There's outside seating during summer. Parking for customers.

Elizabethan Restaurant

Crown Square, Matlock. Tel (01629) 581180
Grid ref: 297603
Open: Daily 10-6 (summer), 10-4 (winter)

Food: Breakfast menu served all day, including continental and English. Plus sandwiches and baps, toasties and filled croissants, plus main meals including steaks, gammon and mixed grill. Traditional roasts are very popular.

Drinks: Coffee is served in mugs or caffetieres, plus a licence allows for wine and spirits to be sold. English Breakfast tea by the pot.

General: Facing the town centre roundabout, this is a regular tea room by day and an Indian restaurant in the evening - 'Bombay Nights' is open 6pm-midnight daily for sit-down and take-away curries and baltis. Walkers welcome, and dogs also allowed inside. Smoking is permitted in one designated area. Customer toilets are available; but front steps do not allow wheelchair access. Large long stay car

Matlock

park (free) across the river, or short stay car parks up Bank Road (from Crown Square).

Good For You! Matlock

Good for You!

Firs Parade, Matlock. Tel (01629) 584304
Grid ref: 302604
Open: 10.30-3.30 Tues-Sat (for meals) and 10.30-4.30 Tues-Sat (shop, drinks and cakes). Closed for two weeks in August.

Food: Large and adventurous vegetarian and vegan blackboard menu, with a strong leaning towards world food - Mexican, Indian, Spanish, etc. From Veggie breakfast and 'Big Sandwiches' to homemade sweets such as date crumble and sultana halva, with many meals vegan and gluten-free. Plenty of appetising children's choices (and not a chicken nugget in sight!), and a changing specials board.

Drinks: Fair Trade teas and coffees, herbal and fruit infusions, plus unusual selections such as sparkling nettle ale, and real dandelion and burdock.

General: Located at the very top of Firs Parade on the corner with New Street, the café occupies a huge, first floor room above shops and is an official information centre for the Vegetarian Society, as well as being a member of their Food and Drink Guild. The café is easy-going and open-plan, with a particular emphasis on children and families - toys and playthings are always available, and storytelling takes place every third Thursday of the month. There are individually painted chairs, easy chairs and high chairs, and the plants, laid-back music and various carvings and ethnic masks make it a very relaxed venue. Good for You! also includes a wholefood shop, incorporating much of the stock once sold by Beanos of Matlock Bath. No smoking and no dogs. Toilets available. Upstairs location so no wheelchair access. Parking in adjoining streets or short stay car parks.

Coffee Grinder, Regent House, Matlock

Regent House

35 Dale Road, Matlock. Tel (01629) 583660
Grid ref: 297602
Open: Daily 8-5.30 (Mon-Sat), 10-5.30 (Sun).
Food: Range of snacks, sandwiches and sweets, including bagels, warm croissants, oatcakes, filled ciabattas and baguettes (ham and Emmental cheese, local blue stilton with celery and apple, etc). Popular dishes include cheesy scrambled egg with smoked ham on a bagel, plus there's a regular specials board.

Drinks: Coffee comes in cafetières, and the impressive choice includes Sumatron Tiger (sweet and powerful) and Colombian San Agustin, Indian Mysore (full and rich) and Mexcian Chiapas (mellow and mild). The specialist teas include Kenya Subukia

Estate (spicy and aromatic), Black Dragon Choice Oolong and Keemun Mao Feng Finest (intensely malty). Or you could opt or the Early Grey Citrus Special or Singbulli (second flush Darjeeling). English Breakfast Tea is also served!

General: Comfortable, upmarket tea room offering a specialist selection of teas and coffees. The three separate rooms are decorated with plush carpets and tasteful furniture, and welcome families (high chair available), walkers (please leave dirty boots at entrance) and wheelchair visitors (pavement level throughout, and accessible toilets). Check out the antique cash till, weighing scales and the American made coffee grinder on the main counter at the front of the shop. They also sell cafetières, tea strainers and stove top espresso makers. The various off-sales include China Rose tea (very sweet and fragrant) and Indian Monsooned Malabar coffee (very dark and rich). Smoking is allowed. No dogs. Papers for browsing. Parking in free long stay car park off Dale Road near Matlock Bridge, or in short stay car park behind parade of shops. (And for a decent deli there's the Derbyshire Larder across the road from Regent House.)

Riverside Café

Matlock Antiques & Collectables, 7 Dale Road, Matlock. Tel (01629) 760808
Grid ref: 297602
Open: Daily 10-5 (summer), 10-4 (winter).

Food: Filled cobs (hot and cold), toasted sandwiches, jacket potatoes and hot filled pitta bread, plus home-made chilli, soup, pies, 'salad bowl', etc, plus the usual scones and toasted teacakes.

Drinks: Teas include camomile and Earl Grey. Mugs or cups of instant coffee. Plus beer and wine available with meals.

General: Small corner room at rear of Matlock Antiques and Collectables, a sprawling and engrossing series of show-rooms featuring over 70 dealers selling books, linen, furniture, china, jewellery, pictures, clocks, etc. Seven inside tables, but in summer there's more seating on the terrace overlooking the River Derwent. Smoking permitted inside. Dogs outside only; customer toilets. Café (only) accessi-

ble for wheelchair visitors. Papers and magazines to browse. Either park free in long stay car park near bridge, or in short stay car park, around back of shops by river.

> *"Food is an important part of a balanced diet."* Fran Lebowitz

MATLOCK BATH - Derbyshire

Matlock Bath is a peculiar sort of place. Although it's technically outside the Peak National Park, it most definitely feels like the Peak District, with the huge limestone cliffs towering over the River Derwent. Lining the main parade are fish and chip shops and amusement arcades, while above, cable cars glide up to a mini theme park high on the hillside. On sunny weekends and bank holidays it gets very busy. On Sundays in particular, the 'resort' has long been a destination for motorcyclists. They stroll along The Parade, weighing-up each others' machines, in between stops for fish and chips etc. To cater for this there are numerous take-aways and fast food outlets, none of which really fall into to the café or tea room category. Neither do the various cafeterias and restaurants, such as the Old Museum Restaurant and Rose Cottage, and the café bars such as the Old Bank. Matlock Bath, it would seem, is a place unto itself.

Simpsons, Matlock Bath

Matlock Bath – Monsal Head

Simpsons

14 North Parade, Matlock Bath.
Tel (01629) 580504
Grid ref: 297585
Open: 10.30 to mid afternoon (weekends only) in winter, and daily 'till late afternoon/early evening in summer.

Food: Light snacks such as baguettes, toasted teacakes, home-made scones, and hot meals such as custom-made pizza, pasta, etc, with daily specials such as spaghetti and lasagne (the owner has Italian ancestry, in case you're wondering). There are cakes and desserts, such as sticky toffee, and apricot and cream cheese, as well as pancakes and ice cream sundaes.

Drinks: Filter coffee, espresso, double espresso, latte, mocha, cappuccino - plus hazelnut cappuccino and coconut cappuccino. Teas include Earl Grey and Assam, and there's lemon, ginger, and peppermint infusions. The hot chocolate choices feature amongst other things, white chocolate with whipped cream, and banana chocolate steamer.

General: Stylish looking café at the northern end of the riverside parade, near the turning for the station. It has a continental feel, with large potted plants, chequered design flooring, various false archways and stylish prints on the walls. Table service, seats 32, and is available for private functions when a separate menu is available. Piped music. No dogs inside. Steps to toilets (although café itself is wheelchair accessible).

> Hotel Waiter: What would you like?
> George: Tea.
> Hotel Waiter: Earl Grey or Lapsang Souchong?
> George: No, tea.
> From the 1986 film 'Mona Lisa'

MONSAL HEAD - Derbyshire

High above the valley of the River Wye, north west of Bakewell, this location offers stunning views down to and across the famous railway viaduct, with the river winding below. The café is next to the pub/hotel, and there are few finer views on a sunny day.

Monsal View Café, Monsal Head

Monsal View Café

Monsal Head. Tel (01629) 640346
Grid ref: 185715
Open: Daily 10.30-5. From Nov-end March closed Thurs, but not school holidays. Early Dec open weekends only, and closed most of Jan.

Food: Main meals feature ocean pie and keema curry, through to roast of the day and giant filled Yorkshire Puddings. Vegetarian options always available, plus jacket potatoes, Ploughman's lunch, sandwiches, and cream teas. Home-made cakes include Victoria jam sponge, sultana and walnut, apricot and cherry, bread pudding and flapjack.

Drinks: Licenced for alcoholic drinks, plus filter coffee and teas, such as Darjeeling, Earl Grey and lemon.

General: A café of many years standing, it commands a great position overlooking the dale, and with outside seating and a useful serving hatch it's not surprisingly very popular with walkers. Inside there's a certain period feel to the old cottage, although it's spacious if rather rambling, full of memorabilia and fascinating old prints of the area. Originally the building served as the pay office for the navvies constructing the railway through the dale below. At that time it had a tin roof and a wooden frontage. Wheelchair accessible, as is the toilet. No dogs inside, and no smoking. High chair available. Local books, maps and landscape prints for sale. Small pay-and-display car park above dale, and large one behind pub.

Northern Tea Merchants -
tea and coffee for the connoisseur

It has to be said that Chesterfield is a few miles outside the Peak District, but for devotees of high quality tea and coffee the busy Derbyshire town includes a very special venue. Northern Tea Merchants are located on the Chesterfield Road (the A619 from Baslow) approaching but not in the town centre, and since 1959 this privately owned independent family business has been selling a wide range of top notch tea and coffee.

In fact the present proprietor's father founded the Spire Tea Company as far back as 1926, and in 1971 it amalgamated with Northern Tea Merchants. They blend and pack their own tea, as well as roast and grind their own coffee, and supply a wide range of outlets across the region (including several tea shops listed in this book). From their handsome, period shop the speciality and house blends are sold across the counter, and as far as tea is concerned among the former are Ceylon Orange Pekoe, Keemun, Jasmine, Russian Caravan and Gunpowder tea ("a slightly fruity flavour and the best grade of China green tea"). To help you choose there are background notes for each leaf; or you can opt for one of the various house blends that are available in tea bags.

All their coffees are pure Arabian coffees, which can be purchased as whole beans or ground to order. Although there is a very good house blend, you can choose different beans to make your own blends, and among the many, many choices are: Kenya Peaberry, Mocha Dijimmah, Peru Chanchamayo and Costa Rica Re Orosi. Northern Tea Merchants is a fascinating and bewitching place for anyone interested in more than just your bog standard supermarket teabag or instant coffee. Better still, they also have a smart café area with a row of traditional 'tasting bars', plus there are tables with different types of leaves and beans laid out beneath their glass tops. There are as many as 50 different teas and freshly ground coffees available for you to try, while the shop sells a range of tea and coffee-making accessories. Northern Tea Merchants are also licenced importers, packers and wholesalers of Fair Trade tea and coffee.

Northern Tea Merchants
Crown House
193 Chatsworth Road
Chesterfield
Derbyshire S40 2BA
Tel 01246 232600
www.northern-tea.com
E-mail: enquiries@northern-tea.com
Café is open Mon-Sat, 9-5.30pm.

MONYASH- Derbyshire

This former lead mining village once had its own Barmote Court, a special court which administered local mining interests and operated outside conventional day to day law. Although the industry has now vanished, there are various pits and grassed-over mounds in the surrounding fields that indicate where the 'rakes' were once dug. A mile or so north east of Monyash, on a quiet country lane, you will find Magpie Mine, preserved by the Peak District Mines Historical Society, and now a now a scheduled ancient monument. Here is the evidence of 200 years of mining - including the former engine house, chimneys and the more recent winding gear. It's a salutary reminder of what was an exceptionally hard and difficult industry.

Today Monyash is especially popular with walkers and cyclists, situated on the Limestone Way and close to Lathkill Dale and the High Peak Trail.

Ed Driscoll, The Old Smithy, Monyash

Old Smithy Tearooms

The Green, Church Street, Monyash.
Tel (01629) 814510
Grid ref: 150666
Open: 10.30-5 (Mon-Fri), 9-6/7 weekends (summer) and 9-5 weekends (winter).
Food: Wide choice of hot snacks (soup, hot baps, toasties, burgers, eggs) and filled sandwiches and rolls, through to popular main meals: fish and chips, steak wich, omelette, all-day breakfast - including vegetarian or 'Smithy's Breakfast - The

Works!' (bacon, sausage, egg, oatcake, mushrooms, toast, tomatoes and beans). Also see daily specials board, children's choices, ice cream by the scoop, and home-baked scones and apple pie, plus the usual slices, teacakes, etc.
Drinks: Tea, instant coffee, Bovril 'by the mug' (as well as pots of tea), plus milk shakes and a range of cold drinks.
General: Attractive and unspoilt former blacksmith's workshop on the village green next to the pub. The high-ceilinged white-walled main room retains its stone floor and contains a working stove, and it's adorned with various musical instruments and mementoes that reflect the owner's musical tastes (Ed's an accomplished folk musician, and his group can be hired to provide musical accompaniment for private evening functions at the Old Smithy). Seating for 23, but there's a couple of picnic benches out the front, and in summer everyone spills out on to the green opposite. Very popular with all outdoor types - a sign by the door proclaims 'Muddy boots welcome'. Dogs allowed inside; customer toilet at back. Fully wheelchair accessible. Roadside parking, or free public car park on Church Street nearby.

> *"I have a great diet. You're allowed to eat anything you want, but you must eat it with naked fat people."* Ed Bluestone

PILSLEY- Derbyshire

Pilsley is a small estate village on the north western edge of Chatsworth, and the Stud Farm Pantry is part of a stud farm built in 1910 by the 9th Duke of Devonshire for breeding shire horses, to work on his estate. The shire horses disappeared in the 1940s, but in 1977 the Duchess converted the site to a Farm Shop, which has since proved very popular and successful. The premises have been extended for 2003. A coffee shop was also established in what used to be the milking parlour for the pedigree Jersey cattle, and in 2001 was entirely refurbished, so that today you can sit inside or out and enjoy views over Edensor and Chatsworth Park.

Stud Farm Pantry

Chatsworth Farm Shop, Pilsley. Tel (01246) 583392 www.chatsworth.org
Grid ref: 244707
Open: Mon-Sat 9.30-4.45, Sun 11-4.45 all year round (but closes around 4.30 in winter)

Food: Until 11am you can enjoy the 'Duchess' Breakfast' (fresh grapefruit, specially-made muesli, toasted cracked wheat loaf, coffee) or 'All-day elevenses'. Lunch features soups and salad (quiche, smoked mackerel, salmon, oatcakes, etc), rolls and sandwiches, and the highlight of 'From the Bakery' are the mouth-watering cherry sultana scones and butter. The cakes and desserts menu takes up a whole page and includes Victoria sponge cake, 'Passionate' carrot cake, banana and walnut cake, plus treacle and almond tart, bread and butter pudding, Irish cream torte and sticky toffee pudding. As befits the Farm Shop next door, all the produce is fresh and well-made.

Drinks: Freshly-ground coffee (Kenyan, Colombian, decaffeinated), espresso, hot chocolate topped with cream, English breakfast and herbal infusions.

General: A smart, bright ground floor room, with light pine floor and good views from the wide window. Smoking and dogs are not allowed inside, but weather permitting you can sit outside. Table service. Toilets are located elsewhere in the main building. Car park by nearby farm shop for customers.

ROWSLEY- Derbyshire

The Country Parlour enjoys a lovely setting overlooking the riverside meadows at Caudwell's Mill, off the centre of Rowsley. Built in 1874, the water-powered flour mill uses huge steel rollers rather than traditional millstones to grind the flour, and now fully restored it's one of the last of its kind still operating in the country. Today it even sells its own flour, which includes wholemeal, white French, pinhead oatmeal, coarse golden brown and malted flake. As well as the old mill the site includes craft shops, an iron forge, glassblower, jewellery-maker, and so on. Opposite the tea room is a small strip of land that is sown with the likes of wheat and barley by local school children. Away from Caudwell's Mill the handsome Peacock Hotel (dating from 1652) on the main square serves morning coffees and afternoon teas, but beware crossing the busy A6. Beyond the Grouse and Claret pub is a retail area called Peak Village where refreshments are also available.

Flour for sale, Cauldwell's Mill, Rowsley

Country Parlour

Caudwell's Mill, Rowsley. Tel (01629) 733185
Grid ref: 256657
Open: Daily 10-5.30 (10-4.30 Nov-April)

Food: Appetising selection of hot and cold vegetarian food, plus vegan and usually gluten-free options. Nearly everything is home-made, including soups such as leek and potato, pea and mint, curried parsnip, scones and cakes (Derbyshire apple and cinnamon cake, carrot cake, etc) and their popular homity pie. Another favourite is the Miller's Lunch, an open roll with salad that comes in a choice of fillings, including cheddar and apricot chutney, Wensleydale and roasted red peppers, and cottage cheese and pineapple.

Drinks: Over a dozen herbal tea infusions, plus the usual choice of filter coffee, cappuccino, latte, espresso, etc.

General: The long, low tea room at Caudwell's Mill, which was built almost ten years ago, derived its tables and beams from a Scottish mill, its flagstone floor from local cottages, and its distinctive pew-like benches from an old chapel at Crich Carr, near Matlock. It's warm and cosy inside, where well-behaved dogs are welcome, but smoking is not permitted. Since it's all on ground level wheelchair access is possible. The toilet block is 50 yards away, behind the main shop and does not have disabled facilities. Inside seating only; walkers and cyclists welcome (bin bags provided as seat covers for the really muddy!). Car park for mill and café customers (follow signs).

Some types of speciality teas -

Assam: from the state of the same name in Northeast India. This tea has a strong, biting flavour and produces a dark brown liquor. Best served with milk.

Ceylon: produced in what is now Sri Lanka. Highly flavoured and often used to improve taste in blends.

Darjeeling: tea grown in this specific mountain area of India, at an altitude of around 6000 feet, producing a unique, full-bodied flavour with a subtle aroma. It's ideal as an afternoon tea, or as a lunchtime refreshment.

Earl Grey: named after English Prime Minister Earl Grey (1764-1845), and according to legend originally given to him by a Chinese Mandarin seeking influence over trading routes. Served black, it's a smoky tea with a hint of sweetness and usually a blend of black teas and bergamot oil. Earl Grey is the second most popular tea in the world today.

English Breakfast: a blend of Assam and Ceylon teas, and may include Keemun tea. It has been suggested that Keemun tea with milk creates an aroma reminiscent of hot toast - hence the name? Alternatively it could be that the strongly flavoured tea is the ideal brew to start the day. It can be served with milk or lemon, and may also be used to brew iced tea.

Formosa Oolong: Oolong was originally grown in the Fukien province of China, but now the best quality is grown in Taiwan (formerly Formosa). It is partly fermented before being dried, and has a distinctive peachy taste.

Gunpowder Tea: this is the best grade of China green tea. Each leaf is rolled into a pellet, hence the name. Served without milk. Green teas are mostly used in the Japanese tea ceremony, an occasion far removed from the western idea of 'afternoon tea'.

Irish Breakfast: brewed very strong (an Irish saying has it that a 'proper' cup of tea should be 'strong enough for a mouse to trot on!). It's usually blended from an Assam tea base and is served with milk.

Jasmine: a blend of large leaf China teas containing Jasmine flowers. Best served without milk.

Keemun: the most famous of the China black teas, a large leaf tea producing a light coloured liquor. It is said to contain less tannin than other teas, and is a good introduction to the 'novice' tea drinker. It has a mellow and subtle flavour and is served black or with milk.

Kenya: a highly sought after tea because of its clean, crisp flavour and beautiful bright liquor. Used on its own or to add flavour to blends. Served with or without milk.

Lapsang Souchong: a large leaf China tea, it has a wonderful 'smoky' aroma and flavour. Best served without milk.

Russian Caravan: a blend created in imperial Russia from teas brought overland from Asia, and usually a combination of China and India black teas. Served with milk and sugar. Russians prefer very sweet tea, and may add honey and even jam.

(Acknowledgement: Some of the above information kindly supplied by Northern Tea Merchants.)

STONEY MIDDLETON- Derbyshire

'Stoney' dates back to Roman times, when it is believed that a thermal bath was established. The spring still exists on the quiet back lane near the parish church of St Martin. The latter is a curious octagonal affair, built by Joan Padley in the 15th century after her husband's safe return from the Battle of Agincourt, and is said to be the only octagonal church in the country.

June and Glen, Lovers Leap Café

Lovers Leap Café

The Dale, Stoney Middleton.
Tel (01433) 630300 www.loversleap.uk.com
Grid ref: 228756
Open: 8-5.30, Fri-Sat, 9-6 Sun and Bank Hols.
Food: Straightforward good value menu featuring all-day breakfast (includes black pudding, hash browns etc) and light grills, jacket potatoes, sandwiches, toast, scones and a selection of cakes. There's also toasties, omelettes, etc. A specials board has items such as hot roast pork baguette with apple sauce, and home-made lemon tart with vanilla cream. The emphasis is on home-made food where possible and the use of local produce.
Drinks: Tea by the pot or pint mug and coffee in cups or mugs. The café is also licenced for alcohol sales.
General: Recently re-opened, the café sits in a terraced row of cottages on the main road (A623) beneath towering limestone cliffs. The Lovers Leap café has been something of an institution with generations of climbers, walkers, cyclists and cavers. After lying empty for some time, it is good to see the building restored to its former use. The simple character of the original café has been retained, but new

furniture and table coverings give it a brighter feel. The interesting old photographs and newspaper clippings have also been kept. There's a few seats on the pavement outside, but it's noisy and you're very close to the traffic, however there are plans to open a garden adjacent to the building. Walkers, climbers, cavers, and cyclists are still very welcome. Whilst the café is wheelchair accessible, the toilets are not. Well behaved dogs are allowed inside. Parking in lay-by 100 yards up the road. The café turns into a Bistro, Thurs-Sat evenings, opening 7pm to midnight. There is a set menu, which changes seasonally. Bottled beers, wines and spirits available. It is normally necessary to book for the evening.

Lovers Leap Inn, closed in the 1930s

The building was previously used as a pub called Lovers Leap Inn. This closed in the 1930s since when it has been a café. It is named after a celebrated incident, rooted in Stoney's folklore, that took place on this spot over 300 years ago. Local girl Hannah Baddaley, jilted by her lover William Barnsley and in a fit of despair, threw herself off the cliffs above where the café now sits. Luckily her woollen petticoats billowed out, and it is said she parachuted down to the ground safely. Apparently this cured her desire for the chap (well it would, wouldn't it?) and she went on to live to an old age.

> *'Five and twenty ponies Trotting through the dark; Brandy for the Parson, Baccy for the Clerk, Laces for a lady, letters for a spy, And watch the wall, my darling, While the gentlemen go by'.*
>
> English tea smuggler's ballad (1700)

A Short History of Coffee

Inevitably there are numerous stories relating the origin of coffee. One of the most popular concerns an Ethiopian goatherd called Kaldi (around 800AD), who noticed that his animals were getting decidedly frisky after eating the cherry-red berries of a particular shrub. He tried them himself and found they had the same effect. A passing monk, who wanted to stay alert through his long hours of prayer, was also interested in the berry - the coffee shrub - and crushing a few into a powder then poured boiling water over them to make a drink. This, it is said, was the very first cup of coffee.

It was at least a couple of centuries later before the coffee bean was first roasted, by which time the drink was already popular throughout Arabia and its cultivation was closely guarded. In the 1470s Ottoman Turks introduced coffee to Turkey, and the first coffee shop opened in Constantinople (renamed Istanbul) in 1475. Soon there were hundreds around the city, acting as a focus for conversation, music, tales, chess, and so on - they became known as the 'Schools of the Wise'. During the next couple of centuries coffee and the trade in beans slowly spread throughout southern/central Europe, but in fact the first coffee house to open in Europe was in Oxford, opened by a Turkish Jew named Jacob in 1650. Coffee houses began appearing in London and Paris, although Louis XIV still famously preferred hot chocolate! In 1683 the first coffee house opened in Vienna, and here they began refining and sweetening the product, and adding a dash of milk - hence the Viennese coffee.

Coffee houses reached their zenith in the late 17th and 18th century. In England they were crowded and noisy, popular with intellectuals, artists and political activists (they were known as 'penny universities', since that was the price of a cup of coffee). In 1822, a Frenchman invented a machine that forced the hot water through the coffee grounds using steam, rather than let the water simply drip through - the first espresso machine.

Although coffee had entered North America in the early 1600s, tea remained the most popular drink until the Boston Tea Party in 1773, after which Americans began switching to coffee as the 'patriotic' anti-British drink! Meanwhile, the overseas colonies of the Dutch (Sri Lanka and Java) and the French (Martinique in the Caribbean) became key centres of coffee cultivation, which later spread to the huge plantations of Latin America and Brazil. This enabled coffee to be exported in vast quantities to a thirsty public, all over the world.

TIDESWELL- Derbyshire

'Tidza' is a lively and attractive village, nestling in a valley five miles east of Buxton, and probably deriving its name from 'Tidi's stream'. It still manages to retain a good few local shops and pubs, and there are some fine period buildings intersected by occasional 'gennels' (narrow walkways). However, Tideswell is especially noted for its sizeable, 14th-century parish church. Crowned by a hefty Perpendicular-style tower (actually added some time later), it's rather inevitably become known as the 'Cathedral of the Peak'. Among the monuments inside the Church of St John the Baptist is one to Bishop Robert Pursglove, a local lad and who during the 16th century became an important local benefactor. The village primary school is named after him.

> *'Part of the secret of success in life is to eat what you like and let the food fight it out inside'.* Mark Twain

Hills 'n' Dales

Queen Street, Tideswell. Tel (01298) 871519
Grid ref: 153755
Open: Fri-Sun 10-5, all year round
Food: Light snacks such as soup and roll, sandwiches and toasties, jacket potatoes and cream teas. Hot Sunday lunches also served (booking advisable). Home-made cakes and desserts include syrup tart, carrot and fruit cake, plus sherry trifle, pecan pie and bilberry pie. Bradwells ice cream also served, plus take-away scoops.
Drinks: Speciality teas include Earl Grey, Assam and Darjeeling, plus filter coffee (and decaffeinated and cappuccino). There's also Bovril and Horlicks, and milkshakes in strawberry, banana, chocolate, raspberry and pineapple flavours. Hills 'n' Dales is also licenced to serve wine, beer and spirits with meals.
General: Located on the main street opposite the bus stop and public toilets. The café comprises one main room, incorporating a gift shop selling books, prints, cards and souvenirs, plus a small overspill room where dogs are permitted. No smoking throughout the premises. It's a comfortable, carpeted place, with a dozen tables (waitress service) and popular with walkers and other visitors. There are a few outside tables in the summer. Wheelchair access is possible through double doors, and the toilet is also wheelchair accessible. Car parking on adjacent road.

TISSINGTON- Derbyshire

A neat and prim estate village, off the A515 north of Ashbourne, belonging to the Fitzherbert family of Tissington Hall. It's claimed that the first well dressing in the Peak District took place here in 1350, when grateful villagers gave thanks to their springs that they believed had spared them from the plague. These days Tissington welldressing is a major event in the village calendar, taking place on Ascension Day, when up to six wells are decorated. The actual dressings themselves comprise large wooden boards, soaked in water and covered in treated clay, then elaborately decorated with an array of flower petals and other natural products that are carefully pressed into the soft clay to form intricate patterns. Preparation takes many hours, of course, and each design tells its own particular story. As with all the other villages across the Peak District that have similar events, the welldressings stay up for as long as a week afterwards, when dressers hope that the weather won't get too hot (causing the clay to dry out and crack) or too wet (washing the designs away!).

Melissa, The Old Coach House

Old Coach House

Tissington. Tel (01335) 350501

Grid ref: 176523

Open: Daily 11-5 (summer), weekends only in winter (occasional weekdays)

Food: Choice of snacks and hot specials, all prepared in kitchen on premises: from filled baps (including Hartington stilton, cooked ham) and large crispy baguettes (BLT, hot roast beef, etc) to home made soups such as parsnip, and broccoli and stilton. Ploughman's lunch, Sunday roast, pies and stews, through to cakes, scones and home baked puddings (butterscotch fruit and nut tart, apple pie, Bakewell tart). Lunches served 11-3, afternoon tea from 3-5.

Drinks: Columbian ground coffee (mug or cup), cappuccino, latte, espresso, mocha; teas include Earl Grey, Assam, Darjeeling and fruit/herbal infusions; hot chocolate with whipped cream or topped with flake; and cold drinks including fruit presse.

General: Award-winning renovated coach house in the pretty estate village of Tissington. The high arched ceilings, flagged floor and two huge, smoked glass windows give the long room a feeling of space and elegance. There are ten tables, with popular outside seating in summer; children are welcome, and they have their own, well-thought out menu. Orders are taken at the main counter, then food is brought to the table. Walkers are welcome. No dogs or smoking inside. Background music. Fully wheelchair accessible, including smart toilets. The small gift shop sells candles made from the nearby village candleworks. Free parking in road outside (not during well-dressing), or a short distance away in Tissington Trail car park.

UPPER HULME - Staffordshire

The Roaches Tea Room at Paddock Farm is located on the lane beyond the village of Upper Hulme, which itself is off the A53 (Buxton-Leek road) on the far south western edge of the Peak National Park. The tea room is named after a spectacular series of gritstone outcrops which rise nearby. The serrated and weathered shapes provide an eye-catching feature for miles around. Long popular with climbers, it's also possible to follow paths around and across the top of the rocks, from where there are panoramic views towards Leek and Tittesworth Reservoir. The Roaches are believed to be named after the French word 'rocher', literally meaning rock, and were named by French monks who once had an abbey nearby.

Sign at Roaches Tea Room

Roaches Tea Room

Paddock Farm, Upper Hulme.

Tel (01538) 300345

Grid ref: 006613

Open: Daily 9-5.30, except Tues.

Closed Dec-Feb.

Food: Soup, hot baps, sandwiches, salads, ploughman's, toasties and scones, plus Staffordshire oatcakes with cheese (you're now in Staffordshire, not Derbyshire!). Everything is sourced locally and made fresh on the premises, including the wide range of cakes and desserts (raspberry sponge, cherry crumble, apricot cake, lemon meringue pie). There's also fruit pies, tea cake, cream teas, and so on, plus a daily specials board with favourites such as casseroles, pies, etc. Traditional roasts are served each Sunday between 12-3 (booking advisable), and the farm has also begun rearing its own stock (lambs and cows at present).

Drinks: Teas include decaffeinated, Earl Grey and Darjeeling, plus herbal infusions (lemon zester, camomile, blackcurrant Bracer, peppermint and strawberry). Rombouts coffee is served by the cup, and includes decaf. Cappuccino and creamy hot chocolate by the mug, plus milk shakes and other cold drinks.

General: Paddock Farm has been serving up teas to walkers, cyclists, climbers and other tourists for over ten years, earning a reputation for decent home-prepared fare. The dark and atmospheric main room is decorated by an elegant mahogany dresser and grandfather clock, and this leads on to the newer conservatory which becomes a delightful sun trap in the summer. There's seating for 40 inside, and plenty more outside, where the terrace benches and tables afford great views across Tittesworth Reservoir. Table service throughout. A ramp provides disabled entry, and a newly-built toilet block the other side of the car park has full wheelchair access. No dogs allowed. No smoking inside.

WETTONMILL- Staffordshire

Located in a lovely spot, by the River Manifold, on a lane between the villages of Wetton and Butterton, 3 miles south west of Hartington.

Wettonmill Tea Rooms

Wettonmill. Tel (01298) 84838
Grid ref: 096562
Open: Daily 10-5 (summer), weekends only (winter) and closed Sat between Dec and Jan.

Food: Small range of freshly prepared sandwiches and cakes, including sausage rolls, pies and pasties. Cakes include fruit, sponge, lemon and orange, and so on. Ice cream scoops in summer, and also a confectionery counter.

Drinks: Speciality teas include Earl Grey and fruit/herbal infusions, filter coffee, and range of cold drinks.

General: A clean, bright and compact building beside the River Manifold at the former mill, catering in particular for the many walkers and cyclists enjoying the

Upper Hulme – Wildboarclough

Manifold Way. Service is at the counter, and there's only a few seats inside, but the place comes into its own during the summer when the outside picnic benches and grassy riverside strip is very popular. Nearby are two National Trust holiday cottages, and there's also a large, free car park. No smoking in the tea room. Dogs allowed. Despite a small front step the building is accessible for wheelchairs, as is the specially built toilet block next door.

WILDBOARCLOUGH - Staffordshire

This isolated hillside farm, out on the south western fringes of the Peak National Park, is to be found on the A54 Buxton-Congleton road near the hamlet of Allgreave, although its postal address is actually Wildboarclough which is further down in the valley bottom.

Blaze Farm Café

Blaze Farm, Wildboarclough.
Tel (01260) 227229
Grid ref: 975676
Open: Daily 10-5 (5.30 at weekends).

Food: Home-made soup, sandwiches and cakes, all freshly made in the kitchen, plus jacket potatoes and the farm's ever-popular fruit scones (baked daily). Also look out for the occasional bread and butter pudding, chocolate cake and lemon meringue pie. Ice cream desserts include knickerbocker glory and 'Chocolate Indulgence', the latter described as slithers of chocolate fudge cake with one scoop of chocolate chip, caramel, toffee and vanilla ice cream, topped with fresh cream, wafers and chocolate sprinkles. Not for the faint hearted or those on a diet.

Drinks: Tea and instant coffee, including

Wildboarclough

frothy (milky) coffee, plus squash and cans of pop.

General: Housed in the farm's former milking 'shippon' (parlour), this small, dark but attractive stone-flagged café still retains original features such as the wooden animal divides and the milk line and cluster. As elsewhere on the farm, there are plenty of informative signs on the walls explaining its history and the day to day running of the farm. Table service, but ice creams should be chosen at the counter. There's only five tables at the moment, but plans are afoot to convert a further room, and outside at the rear there are six picnic tables that provide glorious views across the valley. The present café is not easily accessible for wheelchairs, although the adjoining toilets are adapted. No smoking or dogs inside. Car park on farm.

Hilly Billy Ice Cream

The Waller family have been farming at Blazes (named after the former local charcoal burners) for over three generations, but a few years ago as the problems in the industry nationally began to mount they decided to diversify, and with a substantial grant from DEFRA they threw the farm open to the public. The centrepiece is their Hilly Billy ice cream, using milk from their own dairy herd, which can be bought in cones or to take away in tubs. The 15 original ice cream flavours include white chocolate mountain, Turkish delight, caramel toffee chunk and pistachio and almond, and so popular have they become that a new batch of 100 litres has to be made every five days. In addition to the ice cream and tea room, the 180-acre farm also includes a nature trail, with a picnic bench in case you want to eat your own food, plus a new skyline walk. As its name suggests the route climbs to the top of the ridge above the farm and enjoys stunning views across to, and beyond, the coned peak of Shutlingsloe. The farm is keen to attract families, offering children the chance to watch lambs being born in the Spring, and there's even a 'Cow to Cone' presentation available, showing the recent diversification on the farm and how their delicious ice cream is made.

Read your tea leaves and predict the future

The method is quite simple. Drink a cup of tea and leave enough tea leaves to cover, say, a one pound coin in the bottom of your cup. Hold the cup in your left hand and turn it three times anti-clockwise to spread the leaves around the cup. The cup is read clockwise from the handle, and symbols near the handle show recent events or events about to happen. Meanwhile, symbols at the bottom of the cup stand for your emotions, and the rim of the cup is the happy zone indicating social plans and possibilities.

These are the major symbols to look for: An alligator is a warning. An arrow pointing up means your luck is improving, but pointing down means your luck is bad. A bag predicts a gift, a bed is emotional contentment. A bell means you will hear news about a problem, and a boat means money is arriving. Bone - be careful; Cake - a party; Car - a new job or a powerful sexual symbol; Circle - complete shows that a project will be finished, but broken shows that a project is unfinished. A compass means a change of direction in your life, and an ear says listen out for unexpected opportunities. A lamp indicates an unexpected celebration, a palm tree foretells a creative period, a pear is a good sign for love, and a pirate forecasts adventures. A question mark warns you must be careful, while an upside-down triangle means bad luck.

WIRKSWORTH- Derbyshire

Wirksworth is notable for its large number of interesting and well-preserved old buildings, especially around the parish Church of St Mary. Founded in AD653 and still retaining a rare Anglo Saxon coffin lid, the church is surrounded by a circular churchyard, and every year is the focus for an annual ritual known as 'clypping' when local people link hands and embrace the entire church. The Heritage Centre in Crown Yard (through the arch way opposite the main square) has an excellent display all about the history of the town, including its centuries-old links with lead mining and its connections with the novelist George Eliot, who called it 'Snowfield' in Adam Bede.

Art, Design and Craft Centre Tea Rooms, Wirksworth

Art, Design and Craft Centre Tea Rooms

11 Coldwell Street, Wirksworth.
Tel (01629) 826766
Grid ref: 288540
Open 8-4.30 (Mon-Sat, closed Sun).

Food: Scones, toasted tea cakes, filled baguettes, toasted sandwiches, plus soup and sandwiches, the latter made to order. All the baking is done on the premises, and since they specialise in celebration cakes and catering the quality is very good. The appetising window display typically includes cherry and ginger cake, flapjack, honey and raisin bars, maids of honour, sultana cake and 'wet nellie' (from a Welsh recipe, apparently, and a bit like bread and butter pudding!). But they also make sugar-free cakes, fat-less cakes and vegan cakes to order, and use GM-free flour.

Drinks: Pots of tea (served with fresh milk) include Earl Grey, English Breakfast and fruit varieties, while coffee comes in filter or cafetières, plus there's drinking chocolate and fruit juices.

General: This tiny shop holds just four tables (waitress service), although a couple are put out on the edge of the pavement in summer. However, plenty of people pop in just to purchase the cakes, and to admire the original range of prints, cards and artwork that is on display (and for sale) around the walls and shelves. There is also a wide selection of jams, pickles, preserves, etc. Pavement level allows wheelchair access, but space is tight, and the nearest toilets are the public loos around the corner by the Red Lion, next to a small pay-and-display car park.

Derbyshire Oatcakes

There are many variations on preparing oatcakes, just as there are serving them. Fried with bacon and egg, or a savoury snack with cheese and ham? Perhaps you prefer them smothered in syrup or chocolate?

Ingredients:
For a small quantity: 2 tablespoons oatmeal, 2 tablespoons flour, 1 teaspoon baking powder, pinch of salt, small amount of water to mix.

Method:
Mix the oatmeal, flour and salt with the water to form a thin batter, then add the baking powder immediately prior to cooking. Pour into a hot frying pan and cook like pancakes for a few minutes each side.

Crown Yard Kitchen, Wirksworth

Wirksworth

Crown Yard Kitchen

Crown Yard, Wirksworth. Tel (01629) 822020
Grid ref: 286539
Open: Daily 9-5 (summer), 9-4 (winter), restaurant open Fri and Sat 6.30-9, Sun 6.30-8.30
Food: Imaginative range of meals and snacks, freshly prepared on the premises. Changing blackboard menu and daily specials offer such lunchtime treats as Black Forest smoked ham, four-cheese ravioli, and roast pheasant, as the popular Quarryman's Casserole (warming stew with bread and pickles, plus dessert). Lighter options include jacket potatoes, sandwiches and baguettes, teacakes and scones. Look out for hot puddings such as chocolate sponge and treacle sponge.
Drinks: Apart from filter coffee, expect expertly-made latte, espresso and cappuccino, and hot chocolate with cream. Range of teas, including infusions. Fully licenced.
General: A large, glass-fronted room that is both bright and spacious, and overlooks the courtyard next to Wirksworth's Heritage Centre (entrance opposite Market Place). Its colourful interior - the blue tablecloths complement the white and blue paintwork - is contemporary and even slightly Mediterranean in feel, with fresh flowers, gentle piped music, and browsing newspapers. There are high chairs available, and disabled access via a ramp (toilets next door in Heritage Centre foyer currently involve steps). No dogs inside, but the courtyard tables in summer are very popular with all-comers. Table service. Parking in pay-and-display car park in Market Place. Fri-Sun evenings a full restaurant menu is served, and prior booking is advisable.

Spencers the Bakers

31 St John Street, Wirksworth.
Tel (01629) 825721
Grid ref: 287538
Open: 8.15-5 (Mon-Sat, closed Sun).
Food: Range of light snacks, toast and teacakes, including filled rolls and sandwiches, cheese/beans/eggs on toast, baked potatoes, and breakfast menu (such as bacon rolls). Selections from the bakery feature pasties and pies, scones and tarts, and 'fancy cakes'.

Drinks: Instant and filter coffee (mugs or cups), tea (including Earl Grey) and hot chocolate, plus cold drinks.
General: This single room is at the back of a cosy little bakery on the lower part of Wirksworth's main street. Spencers' main outlet is in Ashbourne, and this small premises in Wirksworth was once a wall paper shop. The dark, low-beamed shopfront leads through to the smart, carpeted room, painted a dark pink, with a handsome marble fire place and pine furniture. Although on pavement level, there are two steps to the toilets at the rear. The table service is attentive and friendly, and it's a popular venue for locals and visitors - especially walkers, who enjoy the takeaway service. No smoking and no dogs.

Those you have loved - Former cafés and tea rooms of the Peak

The pretty village of Alstonefield, near Hartington, once had a tea room in the Old Post Office, and although currently tea room-less there are rumours that a new establishment may be opening soon. Poppies at Tideswell closed its doors a few years ago, as did Muddy Boots at Litton Mill. You could once get a cuppa at Wormhill, while the recently-built Cooper's Café at Edale replaced the far more eye-catching original café, which was constructed from two bolted together railway carriages. There have been other closures across the Peak District, as long-standing proprietors have hung up their tea towels or the financial lure of switching from business to residential use proves too great. This was the case at the café at Over Haddon Craft Centre. The famous Wriggly Tin Café at Miller's Dale, an endearing, corrugated iron shack popular with a generation of walkers and cyclists, closed its doors as this book was being compiled, and at least two other well-known village cafes told us that the present season would be their last and so wished not to be included. As with rural pubs, post offices and village stores, the message seems to be: use them or lose them!

58

Index by location

The Peak District Pub Guide

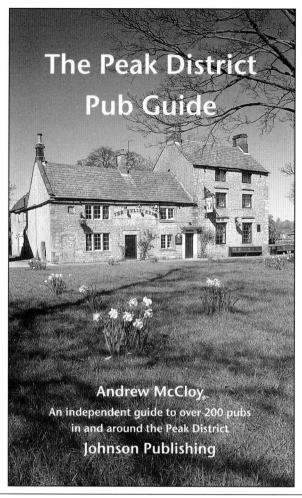

If you've enjoyed the café guide, you may be interested in the twin publication, the Peak District Pub Guide, published in 2002 and reprinted in 2003. Price £4.99. A unique and independent guide to over 200 pubs in and around the National Park. As with the café guide, the pubs are selected entirely on merit, there are no paid-for entries as is the case with many other guides. The book is clearly laid out; for each pub there are details of opening times, beers served, examples of food on offer, whether accommodation is available and finally general points of interest about the pub. There are numerous illustrations throughout the 104 pages. In addition there are related articles of interest to the visitor and resident alike. It is available in selected bookshops, local Tourist Information Centres etc. Alternatively send a cheque for £5.99 (includes post and packing) payable to Johnson Publishing, to 160 Sutton Road, Mansfield, Notts, NG18 5HH.

NOTES

NOTES